Britain's Secret Slaves

Britain's Secret Slaves

An Investigation into the Plight of Overseas Domestic Workers in the United Kingdom

Bridget Anderson

with contributions from
Anti-Slavery International & Kalayaan
and
The Migrant Domestic Workers.

Britain's Secret Slaves
by Bridget Anderson
with contributions from Anti-Slavery International & Kalayaan
and The Migrant Domestic Workers
No 5 in ASI's Human Rights Series – 1993

© Anti-Slavery International
© Kalayaan unpublished personal stories of overseas domestic workers
Editors: Anne-Marie Sharman for Anti-Slavery International
        Dare Kavanagh for Kalayaan
Design: Sue Dransfield
Printed by Whitstable Litho on 100 per cent recycled paper

Photographs:
Cover: The Independent, Peter Macdiarmid
Photos on pp 51 & 58 : The Independent, David Rose
Cartoon on p 83: Commission for Filipino Migrant Workers

British Library Cataloguing in Publication Data
Anderson, Bridget
Britain's Secret Slaves: Investigation into the Plight of Overseas Domestic Workers in the United Kingdom – (Human Rights Series; No. 5)
I. Series
331.6

ISBN 0-900918-29-2

ACKNOWLEDGEMENTS

Anti-Slavery International thanks the European Human Rights Foundation, the Joseph Rowntree Charitable Trust and the Katharine Morton Trust for supporting the publication of this report.

Anti-Slavery International and Kalayaan thank the researchers and writers who have participated in the preparation of this report.

CONTENTS

Foreword by Lord Hylton — 7

International Definitions — 9

Introduction — 11

Chapter 1:   Maids in the Gulf:
Domestic Workers in the Middle East — 13

Chapter 2:   For Two Meals a Day...
Causes and Processes of Migration — 28

Chapter 3:   *Mama's a Maid in London*
Domestic Slavery in the United Kingdom — 41

Chapter 4:   Kalayaan means Freedom!
Campaigning in Britain — 57

Chapter 5:   The Hidden State:
The European Dimension — 71

Chapter 6:   Not Home Yet:
What Needs to be Done — 87

Appendices:

  I.   The Legal Status of Overseas Domestic Workers in the United Kingdom — 95

  II.   Report on Domestic Workers by the Anti-Slavery Society to the United Nations Working Group on Contemporary Forms of Slavery, 1990 — 107

  III.   Information for Domestic Servants Travelling to the United Kingdom: text in Home Office Leaflet, 1991 — 112

  IV.   Letter from the Immigration and Nationality Department to ASI setting out the Home Office position, 1993 — 115

  V.   The Institutions of the European Community — 117

  VI.   Kalayaan Model Contract of Employment for Domestic Workers — 118

FOREWORD

Some five years ago a Radio 4 programme, heard when driving, first alerted me to the existence of domestic slavery in Britain. I wrote to the then Home Secretary and received an emollient answer. In 1990 the High Court award to Mrs Swami of £300,000 in damages for assault, wrongful imprisonment, non-payment of wages, etc. made it clear that the problem remained. I now know that princesses, diplomats, doctors of Medicine and other normally respectable people keep bonded, indentured domestics in virtual slavery and all too often their misdeeds go unchecked. The meetings with Ministers, the Parliamentary debates and questions which I and others have initiated, unfortunately so far have not succeeded in making major improvements in the situation.

Domestics from overseas, nearly all working for foreign employers, and mostly in London and the Home Counties, remain wide open to exploitation. As some leave the country or become free, others arrive. For these reasons, I warmly welcome this book and trust that it will be widely read and lead to effective action. We should uphold the spirit of Lord Mansfield's historic Judgment of 1772, which declared that slavery could not exist in Britain.

It is the particular merit of this book that it sets out local problems in a world-wide context. It explains how grinding poverty in the Philippines, Sri Lanka and some other developing countries, forces workers, both skilled and unskilled, to seek employment overseas. The burden of foreign debts and balance of payment deficits exert similar pressure. Useful chapters also examine the problems and policies affecting migrants in the EC and Canada.

Women, and especially those who are the sole or principal bread-winner in a family, can often see no alternative to working abroad. One million Filipinas are thought to be migrant workers. The majority of them are in the Middle East, from where some thousands have reached England.

Proper protection is urgently needed for all workers whom we admit to this land. I trust that the righting of wrongs on our own door-step will encourage us to strive harder to lessen poverty, injustice and exploitation affecting the whole human family.

Lord Hylton, MA, ARICS
An Independent (Non-party) Member of the House of Lords

INTERNATIONAL DEFINITIONS

From the League of Nations Convention on Slavery, Servitude, Forced Labour and Similar Institutions and Practices (1926):

Slavery is the status or condition of a person over whom any or all of the powers attaching to the right of ownership are exercised.

Article 1 (1)

From the Universal Declaration of Human Rights (1948):

No one shall be held in slavery or servitude; slavery and the slave trade shall be prohibited in all their forms.

Article 4

From the United Nations Supplementary Convention on the Abolition of Slavery, the Slave Trade, and Institutions and Practices Similar to Slavery (1956):

(The following is listed as one of the institutions and practices similar to slavery)

Debt bondage, that is to say, the status or condition arising from a pledge by a debtor of his personal services or of those of a person under his control as security for a debt, if the value of those services as reasonably assessed is not applied towards the liquidation of the debt or the length and nature of those services are not respectively limited and defined.

Article 1 (a)

From the United Nations Convention on the Protection of the Rights of all Migrant Workers and their Families (1990):

No migrant worker or member of his or her family shall be held in slavery or servitude.

Article 11, section 1

INTRODUCTION

This book illustrates one painful but no longer avoidable fact: that slavery has been quietly re-established in Britain, not illegally, but sanctioned by government.

The new slave-holders are the masters and mistresses of overseas domestic workers who have brought their domestic staff with them into this country. Nominally, the slave-holders are 'employers', the domestic workers 'employees'. If we look behind this facade, however, another reality emerges – a reality which we thought had been abolished in 1833.

The UN has updated definitions of slavery to take into account its present-day forms; most recently it has proposed that:

- slavery is any form of dealing with human beings leading to the forced exploitation of their labour;
- slavery is any institution or practice which, by restricting the freedom of the individual, is susceptible of causing severe hardship and serious deprivation of liberty.[1]

Moreover, even the existence of a written contract is not of itself a guarantee that the worker is not in a situation of slavery.[2] It is a matter of record that labour regulations in many overseas states expressly omit the protection of migrant domestic workers. Abuses are therefore common, conspicuously so in the Gulf states[3], and workers frequently find themselves not so much employed as enslaved.

One might suppose that when such workers find themselves accompanying their employers into this country their subjection would be at an end – that, in the words of the poet Cowper:

Slaves cannot breathe in England, if their lungs
Receive our air, that moment they are free;
They touch our country and their shackles fall.[4]

But the British Government has withdrawn from overseas domestic workers entering this country that fundamental freedom without which all worker's rights are meaningless: the right to change employers. Instead of affording these workers the protection of British law as it applies to all others working here, our Government has provided fresh shackles with which to bind them.

Under our system the employers are free to exchange staff at will; the employees depend for their entire livelihood and immigration status on the employer whose name is added to their passport when it is stamped upon entry to the UK. If such tied employment does not of itself authorise slavery, it is obvious that it can facilitate it; and the following pages show that it has.

Exactly how slavery returned to these shores can be understood only in the wider context which this book provides.

Chapter 1 begins with the personal testimony of a victim of the immigration 'concession' our Government makes for the employers' benefit, discusses the devalued and unprotected status of domestic work here as elsewhere, and traces the passage of migrant domestic workers to Britain via the Gulf states.

Chapter 2 broadens the scope of inquiry to consider the effects on individuals, families, nations and economies of labour migration in a world of increasing disparity between the rich and the poor, the North and the South.

Chapter 3 returns to examine in detail the situation that has arisen in Britain, the Home Office concession that lies at its root, and how completely the interests of the workers are disregarded by the State and employers alike.

Chapter 4 stays in Britain to describe the vital work done by voluntary organisations to rebuild shattered lives and broken spirits among the concession's victims, and the growing support for the campaign to afford justice to these migrant workers.

Chapter 5 provides a review of the situation in the European Community, describing the position facing migrant workers in neighbouring countries; and the intergovernmental arrangement to police migrants within the EC.

Chapter 6 looks further afield – to Hong Kong and Canada – to examine the results of their attempts to solve similar problems. This chapter then outlines clear and carefully considered recommendations to prevent and redress the harms arising under our own, as yet ad hoc, system.

But running throughout this book, and unlikely to be forgotten by those who come across them, are the heart-breaking and often terrifying stories of the domestic workers themselves – stories of unbearable hardship endured beyond their, and our, notions of contractual labour. Their experiences show that we are not engaged here in a theoretical discussion. Even though this is modern-day slavery with shackles made of passports, not iron, its effects on the human spirit are as of old. The stories of its victims must stir us into action or expose us as a less than civilized and a far from decent nation.

We may have allowed a form of slavery to return to our country unwittingly; we can no longer claim ignorance if we allow it to continue.

---

1. United Nations E/CN.4/Sub.2/1982/20, *Updating of the Report on Slavery Submitted to the Sub-Commission in 1966*, Report by Benjamin Whitaker, Special Rapporteur.
2. In practice, to establish whether the person is suffering appalling working conditions, or is the victim of a form of slavery, several aspects of a labour contract have to be examined, in particular: the kind of work, the working hours and rates of pay, the negotiating capacity, supervision and freedom of movement, whether there is mental and physical abuse, and whether there is the ability to transfer to another employer.
3. See for example "Punishing the Victim: Rape and Mistreatment of Asian Maids in Kuwait", 1992. *Middle East Watch: Women's Rights Project* 4 (8), New York and Washington: Human Rights Watch.
4. Cowper, William 1743 - 1809. The Task, bk. ii, The Timepiece 1.40.

CHAPTER ONE

Maids in the Gulf: Domestic Workers in the Middle East

I was treated as a slave. In the presence of my employers I had to remove my shoes. If they passed me I had to bow. I could never be seated in their presence. They did not use my name, only bad words like 'You, Dog', or 'Donkey', or, if I was close and they wanted something, they just tugged my hair and pointed. The children used to hit me with their toys if I did not do exactly as they wanted.[1]

Alice was twenty five when she left her job as a surveyor for the Ministry of Public Highways in Manila, Philippines. She is a qualified civil engineer, yet her salary was only some 1,500 pesos a month (about £35),[2] not enough to pay for her four brothers and sisters to go through school and cover her own most basic needs. When she saw a recruitment agency advertising posts as civil engineers in Kuwait with a pay of 10,000 pesos a month (about £215), she seized the opportunity.

But the agency's fee for finding a professional post was 21,000 pesos (some £450), half of which had to be paid immediately. Alice's parents mortgaged their small patch of land, and she undertook to repay the rest on taking up her position. Interviewed and accepted she left for Kuwait.

On arrival at the recruitment office in Kuwait City, she was abruptly informed that she could not work as a civil engineer:

Can you iron? Do you know how to clean and how to wash clothes? For Filipinas the work here is domestic. No, you cannot phone the agency in Manila, it is too expensive for long distance. Can you pay your airfare back? Can you pay the agency the fees you owe? No? Then you must sign this contract as domestic servant.

Alice had no choice but to sign the contract, not for £250 a month as a civil engineer as she had been promised but for £120 as a domestic worker.

Her employers were members of the Kuwaiti royal family, and her tasks ranged from child care to waiting at table:

I was up at 5.30 to make breakfast for the children. I could only go to bed after the adults. Since the royal family is different from ordinary people they have lots of friends and entertained regularly until 2am. Midnight was an early night for me. In the two and a half years I was working for them I had no day off, no time off. Once I asked if I could have even one hour to go to church and they said, 'You are not here for pleasure, so you must stay here to work.' Another time I asked them for an evening just to write my letter home, and they told me, 'Well, there are plenty of nights coming but if I tell you you are going to work, you are going to work'. So I didn't have time even to post my salary to my parents, instead I had to ask the driver to do it. The worst time was in the month of Ramadan, when I had to work day and night with no break, only maybe if I could snatch a nap in a chair.

It is very hard to attend to the wishes of the parents and the children at the same time. If the father is shouting and I am having to get something for the child he will get very angry with me, and take my shoulders and shake me. If you don't remove your shoes or slippers they will use embarrassing words, and it's no good saying sorry, they just say, 'In what bank are we going to deposit your sorry? We are spending money. We are paying you to do a job. Why are you not working properly?'.

The Gulf has thousands of similar stories among its estimated 1.2 million domestic workers. Of course, there are tales of success, women who made enough money to pay off their debts, to build a house or to ensure their children went to school, but there are also cases of abuse and extreme exploitation, of rape and beatings, non-payment of wages, physical and mental torture. Even for those who manage to get what they want and need from the Gulf, the cost is often very high.

The women are predominantly from Sri Lanka, Indonesia, India and the Philippines, with Sri Lanka providing the largest proportion of these. Like Alice, they live with their employers, and work for long hours and low wages. Their pay depends on their country of origin: according to figures from the International Labour Organization (ILO), Filipinas receive an average of US$300 (£158) a month, while Sri Lankans and Bangladeshis, at the bottom end of the scale, earn not more than US$170 (£90).[3]

Domestic Labour

Domestic labour, whether performed by maidservants or housewives, is undervalued throughout the world. It is ubiquitous and essential but unacknowledged, it is unending, monotonous and isolated. The ILO defines a domestic worker as someone who carries out household work in private households in return for wages.[4] However, it also typically involves child care and management of the household. This problem of definition reflects the invisibility of domestic work and its lack of social and economic recognition. Although it requires the execution of a wide range of tasks, domestic work is regarded as unskilled, and it is distinguished by low wages, bad working conditions and insecurity. Because it takes place in the home, often away from other workers, and in close, personal contact with the employer, there are no possibilities for collective bargaining. This also makes it difficult to control the hours of work and allows ample opportunities for avoiding labour legislation and ignoring minimum wages. The work goes unrecognised by government and it does not provide prospects for career advancement. Domestic work is, of course, almost always performed by women.

But domestic work is as important as any other. Although it is generally dismissed as unproductive, calculations as to the importance of housework generally put it at over one third of the Gross National Product (GNP). That is, if the market value of the various services performed by houseworkers were calculated in terms of cleaner, child-minder, cook etc., it would, in the case of the United Kingdom for example, constitute 39 per cent of GNP.[5] This is also calculated within the constraint of the fact that housework is poorly paid.

Domestic work is in many ways subsistence labour: it is the necessary prerequisite to other, apparently more productive forms of work. The housewife who 'doesn't work' nevertheless produces:

> her husband with his clean clothes, well-filled stomach and mind freed from the need to provide daily care for his children; the children fed, clothed, loved and chastised.[6]

Freed from the hours of cleaning his own clothes, preparing his own food, rendering habitable his home, and from the onerous responsibilities of child care, he can then go out and earn a living.

Migrant domestic workers free their employers from the household responsibilities. But others must come in to take the migrant's place at her home: grandparents or sisters look after her children, while she flies thousands of miles away to look after another's child. At the same time as a woman in Britain is being liberated from household chores by a migrant domestic, the migrant's sister, friend or mother is adding the migrant's household chores and child care to her own burden. The real costs of migration are often hidden, and it is debatable whether these do not outweigh the benefits. For the migrant herself, the problems associated with domestic work outlined above are compounded when the worker is isolated, subject to restrictive immigration laws, and dependent on her employer to a far greater extent than she would normally be in her own country.

Migration and the Gulf

Domestic workers comprise about 20 per cent of the estimated 6 million migrants upon whom the Gulf states[7] are completely dependent. Exact numbers are difficult to gauge: the labour importing countries are reluctant to advertise the extent of their dependence on foreign workers, while labour exporters do not want to impose registration systems on their nationals going abroad for fear that this would discourage a valuable source of foreign exchange. A serious attempt at monitoring would be extremely complicated. Difficulties arise, for example, in distinguishing between those workers leaving the host country for a holiday, those wishing to renew their work permits, and those leaving for good. Moreover, by their nature, those who work illegally are not included in any official estimate.

Table 1.1

ESTIMATES OF LABOUR AND RATIO OF CITIZENS TO MIGRANTS IN THE ARAB GULF STATES c.1980

STATE			WORKERS	
	Citizens	%	Expatriates	%
Kuwait	109,170	22.4	378,710	77.6
Qatar	10,341	20.6	39,800	79.4
UAE	55,162	17.5	260,049	82.5
Bahrain	98,764	67.5	47,553	32.5[8]
Saudi Arabia	1,262,393	39.3	1,981,810	60.7
Oman	116,500	45.7	137,200	54.3
Total	**1,535,830**	**36.2**	**2,707,922**	**69.8**

Source: Migrant Workers in the Gulf, Dr Roger Owen.
Minority Rights Group Report no.68, September 1985, p.18

The Gulf area has a long migratory tradition. Trade routes through the region between the Mediterranean and the Indian Ocean have been long established and for centuries people have passed through on the holy pilgrimage to Mecca. The large scale import of labour began in the 1930s under British administration. The Persian Gulf area was administered from India, and when oil was discovered, first in Bahrain (1932) and then in Saudi Arabia (1933), Indian workers were brought in to develop the industry. There were three main reasons for this: the indigenous population was very small; women were largely exempted from work other than domestic work; and a rapidly expanding native workforce would have posed political difficulties for the Gulf rulers. However, post war restrictions on migration temporarily halted this movement, and the emerging oil rich nations turned to neighbouring Middle Eastern countries for their labour needs.

The 1973 so-called oil crisis brought unprecedented economic development to the Gulf. 'Petrodollars' flooded in, and the Gulf States embarked on massive construction and infrastructure projects. Even more labour was needed. For all the rhetoric about wanting to reduce dependence on foreign labour this was, at the simplest level, impossible: there were simply not enough local people to carry out this work. There were other factors operating as well: many of the jobs that needed to be filled were low paid and generally undesirable; some were technical jobs requiring specialist skills, and the Gulf did not have the trained people who could take them on; and finally there was no shortage of well paid, high status bureaucratic, administrative and commercial positions reserved for nationals. Meanwhile, the already small local labour force was contracting even more as educational opportunities brought by prosperity delayed the entry of young people into the labour market:

> *For every person or organization which demanded a reduction in dependence on foreign labour there are others who were equally quick to attack any government which tried to prevent them from importing the workers they want. And whenever one group suggested that a simple way out of the problem might be to admit more long-term foreign residents to local citizenship, there were others to point out that such a step would mean a reduction in the economic value of their own privileges. Meanwhile, governments which were little more than the sum of the ruler's family and some important local merchants and notables would bend this way and that to manage an impossible situation.*[9]

By the early 1970s the Gulf region was beginning to turn away from other Arab sources of labour. This was for a variety of reasons: they were anxious to diversify their sources of labour, to avoid a cartel developing among labour exporters which could exercise a serious influence on their economy. Arab workers were more likely than others to involve themselves in internal affairs and pose a political threat. They were also more likely to settle and to bring dependents. Other sources, particularly Asian countries, were cheaper, brought a wider range of skills and had a more formalized and organized approach to the export of labour.

India, Pakistan, Bangladesh, the Republic of Korea, the Philippines and later, Thailand, Sri Lanka and Indonesia, began to send their young people to work in the Middle East (see table on page 18).

The oil crisis which had brought so much prosperity to the Middle East, had only increased the poverty and the difficulties of life in developing countries. Many nations faced serious problems with their balance of payments deficit as the cost of their oil imports rocketed. So, at the same time as the oil-producing countries were looking for labour, the developing nations were looking for foreign exchange. Export of labour through the 'pipeline to the Middle East' was the apparent solution to both problems. Asian construction workers, technicians and engineers came in their hundreds of thousands. Improvements in health and education standards for the indigenous population also required highly qualified and experienced people – nurses, doctors, teachers.... and the very presence of so many migrants generated their own needs, which in turn had to be serviced. One Kuwaiti MP estimated that

Table 1.2
ANNUAL OUTFLOW OF CONTRACT MIGRANT WORKERS TO THE MIDDLE EAST FROM MAJOR ASIAN LABOUR EXPORTING COUNTRIES 1977-1987

Country of Origin	1977	1978	1979	1980	1981	1982	1983	1984	1985	1986	1987
South Asia											
Bangladesh	15,932	22,739	24,209	32,514	53,839	62,186	58,229	55,921	76,785	68,004	54,500
	(98.2)	(99.7)	(98.9)	(96.4)	(96.5)	(99.0)	(98.3)	(98.5)	(98.9)	(99.0)	(99.1)
India[a]	22,900	69,000	171,800	268,200	272,000	224,257	217,971	198,520	160,396	109,234	121,812
						(93.6)	(96.9)	(96.4)	(98.4)	(96.1)	(97.2)
Pakistan	74,589	75,966	82,195	117,187	151,849	141,416	127,616	99,654	87,523	62,390	69,340
	(53.1)	(58.2)	(65.5)	(90.3)	(90.2)	(98.9)	(99.5)	(99.3)	(98.9)	(99.6)	(99.6)
Sri Lanka[b]	na	na	20,980	24,053	47,394	63,522	68,905	na	na	na	na
				(84.0)	(82.6)	(90.0)	(95.0)				
South and East Asia											
Indonesia			7,651	11,501	11,484	9,595	17,899	28,702	48,280	42,142	
			(73.7)	(71.1)	(64.1)	(45.4)	(61.8)	(75.8)	(85.2)	(90.9)	
Rep. Korea	52,247	81,987	99,141	120,535	138,310	151,583	130,776	100,765	72,907	44,753	
	(94.0)	(97.8)	(98.7)	(96.6)	(93.7)	(91.5)	(83.5)	(85.0)	(90.0)	(85.2)	
Philippines	25,721	34,441	73,210	132,044	183,582	211,033	323,414	311,517	266,617	262,758	306,757
	(70.1)	(67.6)	(79.1)	(83.9)	(87.0)	(84.4)	(85.1)	(84.0)	(78.9)	(73.5)	(72.0)
Thailand	3,870	14,215	8,282	20,761	24,638	105,163	64,405	67,430	61,659	74,046	74,921
	(100.0)	(96.6)	(85.5)	(96.6)	(92.1)	(96.9)	(94.1)	(89.9)	(88.5)	(86.4)	(87.8)

a: Breakdown to the Middle East not available for 1977-81
b: ARTEP estimates
Figures in parentheses give percentage of migrant workers to the Middle East out of total migrants to all countries in the world
Source: To The Gulf and Back, Rashid Amjad, United Nations Development Program, New Delhi and International Labour Organisation Asian Employment Program, New Delhi 1989, p.6.

for every 10,000 new migrants you would need 174 additional workers, 14 for education, 25 for health and 135 for the security services.[10]

Workers coming from Asia did not have the same access to contacts as their Arab counterparts. They could not rely on word of mouth and informal contacts, and hundreds of recruiting agencies began to operate in their countries of origin, usually demanding large fees for placements. The relatively high salaries available in the Gulf meant that this was no deterrent.

The region's prosperity also brought an increase in demand for domestic workers. In fact the demand for construction workers began to fall in the mid-1980s because of the falling price of oil and recession in Europe and the US, and it still has not recovered, despite the massive reconstruction being undertaken in Kuwait in the aftermath of the 1991 Gulf War. The demand for domestic workers, which is less closely tied to the price of oil, has, however, continued to increase.

Wealthy families have always employed housemaids, and now they are more generally affordable. But housemaids are not merely a status symbol. The move towards a consumerist lifestyle and the nuclear family concomitant on increased prosperity has added to the domestic burdens: houses are large and meals remain lavish, but the number of women in the household to share these burdens has diminished. There were, however, plenty of 'mobile maids' to take over. An estimated 30,000 Asian women go to work every year as housemaids in Saudi Arabia alone.[11] In 1985, Sri Lankan female domestics accounted for 57 per cent of all migrants to the Middle East.[12] More generally, about 20 per cent of the migrants in the Gulf are female domestic workers, and housemaids form the bulk of the female labour trade in that area.[13]

Life for any migrant, male or female, is heavily restricted and controlled by tight immigration legislation. The particularities of development in the Gulf States meant that their first immigration laws were developed within the framework of labour legislation. Residence permits are contingent on work permits, and work permits are cancelled after a set, short period of unemployment (ranging from one to three months depending on the country). An application for a work permit can only be made on the worker's behalf by a Gulf sponsor, who is usually their employer. It is this sponsor who undertakes the regular renewal of the work permit, and who, together with the authorities, must agree to any change of employer or extension of permit. Migrants are hired for a specific job, specific employer and specific time, and any deviation or extension of this is hedged with difficulties. The immigration laws thus give employers a great deal of power, the more so given the custom that the employer holds their employee's passport to ensure their good behaviour and that they do not run away.

Moreover, citizenship is tightly restricted, usually to those who have a Gulf parent and who have lived in the country for a very long time. Since migrants are usually restricted by 'maximum stay' laws, and by legislation requiring them to renew their permits outside of the country, citizenship and its attendant benefits are unavailable to them. Whatever they have contributed to the country in terms of their labour and expertise, they have no rights to welfare benefits, to own land, to go into business or to have their family join them. Such rights are generally limited to citizens.

Wages are paid on a three tier system, with Europeans earning the most, followed by Arabs, and then Asians. Within that, rates are set at different levels depending on the rates of the country of origin. Bangladeshis are therefore the lowest paid group – simply because they are Bangladeshis.[14]

Labour laws are extremely harsh and only increase the employer's power. During the probationary period a worker can be sacked without notice or reason – disaster for the migrant who has mortgaged the family's land to pay for recruitment and travel costs. Labour organisations, strikes and demonstrations are generally illegal, and those who attempt to dabble in such activities are liable to instant deportation as an 'undesirable' without any legal proceedings or rights of appeal.

The situation of migrant domestic workers is, however, even worse. The minimum protection granted to workers is not applied to domestic servants, who are explicitly excluded from labour legislation. They are regarded, not as workers, but as members of the household. This perception leaves them particularly vulnerable to exploitation, with the employers having no obligations regarding hours, activities and leisure time.

Despite the wide range of activities covered the work is regarded as menial, unskilled and therefore to be minimally compensated. Housemaids are among the lowest paid workers in the Gulf, and yet their work is extremely demanding. Approximately 45 per cent of all Sri Lankan domestic workers for example, have to maintain a household of nine to twenty rooms, and often they are the only worker.[15] Edita worked in Kuwait:

> *So I wake up at 4.30, I started work before five o'clock. Prepare all, I clean all, including car. They have already eleven children, I take care of the children's dress, I wash clothes, I iron clothes, I prepare meals for the children like that. There are clothes that are not fit in the washing machine. I must wash with my bare hands. Then I have no rest hours. There are times that I cannot sleep even one hour. For my one year and a half I have no day off.......*[16]

After this she was joined by a Sri Lankan woman and her workload decreased slightly, but apart from that there was no improvement in their situation:

> *And we are afraid to eat. There are many food, but we are not, we are afraid to eat, because sometimes she is looking for it. We will ask from her, 'Madam, we'll eat this one? Madam, we'll eat this one, madam?' Even though we are very hungry already, we will wait for her whatever, what she will tell us, 'You can eat', like that.*

مؤسسة الكروان للايدى العاملة
THE KARAWAN MANPOWER EST.

P. O. Box 1449
Tel. : 275884
Telex : 9736 NAMAN BN
MANAMA, BAHRAIN.
C. R. 7911

ص . ب : ١٤٤٩
تليفون : ٢٧٥٨٨٤
تلكس : ٩٧٣٦ نمان بحران
المنامة ـ البحرين
س . ت : ٧٩١١

SERVICE AGREEMENT

This agreement is made on 02.04.90
between Mr. .... of .HOUSE.No... ..ROAD.No... .BLOCK.No..
(hereinafter called the EMPLOYER)
and Mr/Mrs./Miss ....
holding FILIPINO Passport No. .... Issued at MANILA on ....
(hereinafter called the EMPLOYEE), hereby it is agreed as follows :

1) THE EMPLOYEE agrees to work for the EMPLOYER in the capacity of HOUSE MAID for a period of TWO years commencing on 02.04.90

2) THE EMPLOYER shall pay the EMPLOYEE a salary at the rate of BD.45/- per month, provided that the EMPLOYEE should work at the time, place and days specified by the EMPLOYER.

3) The EMPLOYEE shall be on a probation period for THREE month(s).

4) The EMPLOYEE shall be entitled to 30 days leave with full pay after completing this contract.

5) The EMPLOYEE shall be entitled to receive free medical treatment at any government hospital and clinic, through the EMPLOYER, provided that the sickness or injury is not caused by the EMPLOYEE himself/herself or through alcohol or drugs and the EMPLOYER is not responsible, in any case, to treat the EMPLOYEE outside the country where he/she works.

6) The EMPLOYEE hereby guarantees to fulfill his/her duties with honesty and to be of good conduct and to keep the secrecy of the EMPLOYER and not to involve himself/herself in any political or internal affair in the Country of his/her work or residence and not to refuse any duties given to him/her or to cause any disturbance among others; otherwise disciplinary action will be taken.

7) The EMPLOYER shall be providing the EMPLOYEE a living accommodation with free electricity and water till the end of this Agreement.

8) Free food shall be provided to the EMPLOYEE by the EMPLOYER.

9) a) The EMPLOYER shall provide the EMPLOYEE passage facilities from the country of origin to the place of work by air Economy Class.

 b) After the completion of this Agreement or on the termination of the EMPLOYEE'S SERVICE by the EMPLOYER not due to the reasons which are stated below in Clause C the EMPLOYER shall repatriate the EMPLOYEE to the country of origin by air Economy Class.

 c) The EMPLOYER forfeits his right to the above clauses A and B and therefore reserves the right to recover from the EMPLOYEE entitlement such as costs of passage and any other expenses incurred in connection with his employment if the EMPLOYEE'S services are terminated for any of the following reasons :
   1) If the EMPLOYEE resigns before the completion of this contract;
   2) If the EMPLOYEE commits breach of the provision of this agreement.

10) In case of death of the EMPLOYEE, it will be the responsibility of the EMPLOYER to send the dead body and personal effects of the deceased at the EMPLOYER'S expenses to the EMPLOYEE'S country of origin.

11) Female domestic (housemaids) duty hours will be unlimited as she will be treated as one of the family house hold. She will not be allowed to go out of the house alone or on her own.

12) Both parties are to abide by the law of the place of work towards each other.

13) Other conditions : There is no holiday for the House Maids, and it is not allowed for the Christian House Maid to ask her employer to give permission for her to go to Church.

14) This agreement is signed by both parties and each will keep a copy.

Example of an agreement between a Filipino Domestic Worker and her Middle Eastern Employer in February 1990. Note clause 6 'not to refuse any duties given him/her' and clauses 11 and 13.

Seventy five percent of domestic workers work between eleven and twenty hours a day, and 90 per cent have no day off. Almost one third work without a contract.[17] Even when they do have a contract it does not necessarily afford them any protection. If workers sign it in Manila, Delhi, or Colombo, they can be presented with a far less favourable one on arrival. Alice's contract substitution was by no means unusual.

Domestic workers in the Middle East almost always live in, making them even more dependent on the employer's goodwill, and breaking down the barrier between work and leisure – if indeed there is any leisure at all. Alice, like the other domestics in the household, always wore a belt which had a buzzer on it:

> *The worst thing is I am carrying always the bell. When they call you they just hit the button and you will run. We each had our number of chimes, so we know which one is wanted. Mine was two. So I hear, 'Ding! Ding', and even if I am sleeping I must get up and go to them. Even at 4 o'clock in the morning, if they want early breakfast, you have to do that...... You have to be at their beck and call. You don't have any time to eat, and anyway, you cannot cook your own food. If they have left food over you are fortunate, but if they don't have leftovers then you just end up drinking tea or coffee.*

One of the problems most frequently cited by the women who work in the Gulf is their isolation. Cultural and linguistic difficulties are compounded as they are frequently not allowed out of the house, or only with an escort; they have no opportunities to socialise or meet with other people from their country, even relatives, unless they are employed by the same household. Any contact with home is commonly withheld by the employer on the grounds that the women might become homesick, depressed or overly concerned about personal matters. Letters and cassettes, both from and to their family, are withheld or destroyed, often without telling the employee, giving rise to a great deal of distress on the part of the women and their families, who have no idea why communication has stopped.

As well as exploitative and oppressive working and living conditions, because of their personalized relationship with their employers, domestics are extremely vulnerable to physical and sexual abuse. Buttressed by immigration legislation and lack of labour protection, encouraged by state practices and policies to regard all migrant labour, and female domestic labour in particular, as inferior and deserving of less respect than citizens, employers subject their housemaids to a range of mental and physical cruelties. Edita's Sri Lankan co-worker was sent back to the agency when she refused to have sex with her employer. But first he whipped her fifteen times with his policeman's belt. Edita herself was beaten unconscious for not attending to his call immediately. Like almost all domestics she was subjected to degrading abuse, and had to answer to the name of 'Pig', 'Donkey', and 'Slave' – terms often used by the children who were in her care. Beatings, by both adults and children are common, as is denial of food, being locked up and spat at, sexual abuse and rape. In one case that came to light in 1990, a Filipina was returned home insane, having had a steam iron applied to her genitals by an irate employer. Such incidents are only the more extreme cases of mental and physical cruelty that have become acceptable in a situation where employers have almost complete control over their employees.

> ## Sheikha's Story
>
> Sheikha, a 30 year old Indian woman, was raped and beaten by her employer, who left bruises on her chest and thighs. After she was raped, Sheikha escaped from the house and walked alone to al-Razi Hospital, where she fainted in the entrance at 6.30am. According to hospital employees, while Sheikha was in the hospital, the employer who allegedly raped her came to the hospital and asked to see her records. He told the hospital staff that she had epilepsy and was bruised when she fell down during a seizure. He said she should be released to his custody when her treatment was completed. Sheikha was afraid to go back and told staff members: 'Maybe they will kill me and then who will take care of my children?' Sheikha was repatriated to India by her embassy in late March. To our knowledge, no action was taken against her employer.[18]

The Gulf War

Despite their large numbers, migrant workers were forgotten during the 1991 Gulf War. An estimated 1.9 million Asians worked in Iraq and Kuwait before the war. They were abandoned by their employers, and by their host government – though there are tales of Bangladeshi workers being forced to dig trenches for Iraqi soldiers. Their own governments, particularly the Philippines, were criticised for failing to evacuate many of their citizens before the war. Even after hostilities began the Philippine Overseas Employment Agency was processing 600 contracts daily for workers bound for Saudi Arabia. Saudi authorities feared mass evacuation would play havoc with their economy and in particular disrupt oil and drilling operations. Saudi Arabian employers were accused of forcing non-Arab workers to remain in the country by withholding passports and tickets. Many migrants were consequently left stranded, were owed thousands of dollars in unpaid wages and benefits and were forced to trek across the desert to refugee camps in Jordan, there to wait in unsanitary conditions with little food, hoping for repatriation.

Teresa worked in Kuwait as a domestic for the Al Sabah family. When news of the Iraqi invasion came, she was with the family and 15 of their 56 servants at a seaside chalet near the border with Saudi Arabia:

> When we heard that war had broken out and our lives were in danger we left for Saudi, the family in their car, and the servants in other cars. But only theirs turned to the Saudi border, and we realised that we were being sent back to the Palace in Kuwait City, that they had left us like dogs.
>
> When I went back I saw there were thousands of servants abandoned in the city, with nothing to eat, drinking from dripping water hydrants. It was pitiful to see the people starving in the streets. There were many Filipinas in the Iraqi embassy, so many that there was not space for a pin between them, because they said the Iraqis were flying them home.
>
> I decided to go to Jordan. There were many people walking through the desert like me, and my companion, another Filipina, died on the way. When we arrived at the camps I couldn't believe the conditions were so terrible, they were indescribable, and so many people dying. We were frightened too that Israel would bomb Jordan, and in the end I decided to contact my employers, because I knew they would be in Geneva, to see if they would take me back.[19]

They did indeed fly her from Jordan to Switzerland, but they abused her so badly, she could bear it no longer. After a particularly severe beating, during which her employer jumped up and down on her stomach, causing her to vomit blood, she decided to run away. Teresa is now an unauthorised worker in Switzerland.

It has been reported that since the end of the Gulf War conditions for domestic workers in Kuwait have significantly worsened. In February 1992 Sri Lankan, Indian and Bangladeshi officials stopped recommending that their citizens travel to Kuwait for work. The Sri Lankan Embassy displays pictures of a housemaid who was beaten and burned with a cigarette and had her hair cut off by her employer. As many as six sexual assault cases are reported each day and at least one pregnancy a month according to Sri Lankan officials. 'What can we do?' says Wica Ramasinghe, Labour Secretary at the embassy, 'There is no protection for these women. They are being treated like slaves. We can't leave them with the Kuwaitis'.

At least one popular Islamic cleric, Abdul Aziz Habeen, has accused Kuwaitis of hypocrisy in condemning the rape of Kuwaiti women by Iraqi soldiers while ignoring the charges of rape of foreign women by Kuwaiti men. In February 1992 there were 69 women hiding in the Sri Lankan Embassy with as many as eight more arriving daily. In March 1992 there were 221 Filipinas hiding in the Philippines' Embassy, nine pregnant and seven others who had been so badly assaulted they were 'mentally disoriented':

> One of them is 31-year old Rodriga. Unable to speak since she was struck repeatedly on her head two weeks ago by her Kuwaiti employer, she now stares straight ahead, rarely makes eye contact, and has to be led around by the hand. Her right eye is black, her left cheek is swollen.

'Our life is worth nothing to the Kuwaitis', said Marife Venezon, 31, who escaped after she says her employer tried to assault her. *'Even the Iraqis didn't treat us this bad.'*[20]

In 1992, several dozen women were also reported to be in the Indian and Bangladeshi embassies, with up to twenty more arriving each day. Most cannot leave the country because they do not have their passports. Kuwait offered to fly home women who alleged they had been abused, but at more than twice the normal airfare, because they had to cover the employers' 'reimbursement fee'.

These are the women who have managed to run away. Possibilities of escape from such abusive situations are negligible. Women have no chance of repaying debts incurred by recruitment fees if they leave the Middle East. As we have seen, it is difficult for women to change employers, and virtually impossible without the permission of her current employer. Those who opt to change employers without consent are in the worst situation of all. Posters offering rewards with photographs of runaways appear on billboards and on television. Very few run the risk of leaping out of the frying pan into the fire.

In recent months, the Philippine Embassy in Kuwait, in addition to providing a refuge for battered escapees, has become an unofficial employment office. Here Kuwaitis and expatriates interview prospective domestic workers and, having made a choice, try to obtain the woman's release, for a fee, from her previous employer: "unless a runaway maid has a release, it is virtually impossible for a new employer to get her a visa that allows her to remain in Kuwait".[21]

While not all jobs lead to rape and sexual abuse, most of them entail mistreatment. Excluded from any protection which could be given by the labour laws, domestic servants have no holidays, no time off -not even to go to church – and no limit to the hours they have to work; as well as their passport, their wages are withheld at least until the employer has recouped the agency fees, if not longer.

Josephine's Story

Richard and Mona Brook went to the Philippine Embassy looking for a domestic; after talking to several women, they decided they would like to hire Josephine, a 23-year-old who had run away from her Kuwaiti employer after his 29-year-old son had hit her and threatened to kill her. Mrs. Brook telephoned offering the employer 300 dinars (£540) to release her. He refused, saying that it had cost him 500 dinars (£898) to recruit her; when Mrs. Brook suggested that, if Josephine was deported, he would lose the money, he answered that it was not the money: as a Kuwaiti in Kuwait, he was going to get her out of the embassy as a matter of principle.[22]

In spite of this, the women try to avoid being sent home, actively looking for new jobs in Kuwait – not easy, given that their ex-employer often has no intention of allowing their release. They do this because they see this as their only hope of earning the money they need to repay the substantial debt to their original recruiters at home.

However, domestic workers are unique in the Middle East in that it is common for them to travel with their employer. Britain has strong business links with the Gulf, and it is also a popular holiday destination. Housework and child care must be done in London as in Bahrain, and so it is that the domestic servants are brought to Britain, and in particular, to London. Most, but not all, the workers who come to Britain in this way are Filipinas, rather than as might be expected, Sri Lankan. This is because Filipino workers are more expensive than Sri Lankans and therefore are hired by wealthier families, who are in turn more likely to travel and spend long periods of time in Britain.

The change in location brings no improvement to the women's situation, indeed it often becomes even worse; because only a few of the household staff may travel with the family, those who do, find themselves with additional child care and entertainment responsibilities to add to their workload. Faced with these intolerable conditions, many take the risk and try to escape. Those women who succeed in running away in Britain are faced with a whole new set of problems. They are now classed as unauthorised workers, with no rights, and are liable to deportation should they be discovered. They must overcome the practical problems of finding work, a place to live and of how to survive in a strange country.

Before looking at the problems faced by these women in Britain however, it is important to consider why they leave their homes and families in the first place in order to understand some of the factors that drive them into slavery.

1 Unless otherwise specified, cases are drawn from the case histories collected by the Commission for Filipino Migrant Workers and Kalayaan. The names of the women have been changed to protect their identity.
2 Where rates of exchange are quoted, they are from the Financial Times World Currencies, 15th September 1992; they are included to give the reader an indication of the relative values.
3 Patricia Weinert, 1991. "Foreign Female Domestic Workers: Help Wanted!" World Employment Programme Working Paper, Geneva: International Labour Office.
4 International Standard Classification of Occupations – ISCO 68:
5-40.20 HOUSEMAID
    Cleans rooms, prepares food and serves meals, washes dishes and performs additional domestic duties in private households: dusts and polishes furniture, sweeps and cleans floors and floor coverings and washes windows; makes beds and changes linen; washes, pares, cuts and otherwise prepares food for cooking or eating raw; prepares beverages, salads and desserts; washes dishes and cleans silverware; sets table and arranges chairs in dining-room and serves food; washes linen and other textiles by hand or machine and mends and irons them, performs additional duties such as answering telephone and doorbell, feeding pets and purchasing food and other supplies. May cook meals, bake cakes and pastries and perform other cooking work.
    Source: International Standard Classification of Occupations. 1968, Geneva: International Labour Office.

5 Wickham M and Young B, 1973. *Home Management and Family Living*. Report of the questionnaire of the Home Economics Sectional Committee, London: National Council of Women.
6 Oakley Ann, 1981. *Subject Women*, Oxford: Martin Robertson.
7 The term 'Gulf States' covers the member countries of the Gulf Cooperation Council (GCC) consisting of Bahrain, Kuwait, Oman, Qatar, Saudi Arabia and United Arab Emirates. The UAE is a federation of seven small sheikdoms consisting of Dubai, Abu-Dhabi, Sharjah, Ajiman, Ras Al-Khauriah, Umm al Aqwain and Fujairah. The term does not cover Iraq or Libya. Though both are oil producing nations which import labour, their problems and polices towards migrant labour are rather different. Very few of the domestic workers who end up in Britain have come via these countries.
8 The amount of oil coming from Bahrain has decreased significantly, and it has diversified its economy more successfully than any other Gulf State, in particular its service sector and its offshore banking facilities. It therefore employs a larger proportion of its indigenous population and fewer migrant workers.
9 Dr Roger Owen, 1985. *Migrant Workers in the Gulf*, Minority Rights Group Report No. 68, London: MRG.
10 Quoted Owen, ibid.
11 *Straits Times*, 31st January 1990.
12 Eelens, F. and Speckmann, J. 1990. "Recruitment of Labour Migrants for the Middle East: the Sri Lankan Case", *International Migration Review*, 24 (2), New York.
13 Brochmann, G. 1990. *The Middle East Avenue: Female Migration from Sri Lanka: Causes and Consequences*, Oslo: Institute for Social Research.
14 Spaan, E. "Socio-Economic Conditions of Sri Lankan Migrant Workers in the Gulf States" in Ed. Eelens, Schampers and Speckmann eds 1992. *Labour Migration to the Middle East – From Sri Lanka to the Gulf*, London: Kegan Paul International.
15 Spaan E., ibid.
16 Anti-Slavery International: unpublished research.
17 Spaan E., ibid.
18 "Punishing the Victim: Rape and Mistreatment of Asian Maids in Kuwait", 1992. *Middle East Watch: Women's Rights Project* 4 (8), New York and Washington: Human Rights Watch.
19 Interview with Old Street Films, June 1991.
20 *USA Today*, 5th March 1992.
21 *The New Yorker*, 16th November 1992.
22 ibid.

CHAPTER TWO

For Two Meals a Day...
Causes and Processes of Migration

Workers have been transferred in large numbers and over long distances since the end of the 15th century, from the enslavement of indigenous people that followed the conquest of the Americas, African slavery, 'coolies', through to the present-day systems.

Master-servant, or even master-slave relationships that have developed over generations within the same geographical areas are generally subjected to constraints. While one would not wish to deny that they are inherently exploitative, the 'master' generally has certain responsibilities and obligations to the 'slave', developed in order to curb excesses that could lead to revolt.[1] The same is not true when servants or slaves are imported from overseas.

Third World domestic workers in the Gulf states and the United Kingdom form part of an estimated 100 million 'people on the move' in the world today. Of these, some 50 million are migrant workers, 30 million of whom are 'irregular', ie undocumented or without legal permission to work. Why do so many people leave their homes and their loved ones behind for such an uncertain future? Debates and theories of migration dispute the relative importance to be given to the different factors in a decision to migrate, but looking at the issue broadly there are three factors operating: the personal decision of the individual migrant; national policies of sending countries; and national economic policies of receiving countries. Personal and national factors operating on the individual's decision to migrate, can also be seen as 'pushing' them to find work overseas. These need not be economic. But equally important are the 'pull' factors: it is almost a truism to discuss the relationship between immigration and the desire for cheap, Third World labour. In the case of domestic work this is operating to the benefit both of the First World female labour force, and the labour importing countries in general.

Migration then is a complex phenomenon. Moreover, it is not necessarily a move from the Third to the First World, but also occurs within countries and continents.

Internal Migration
Travelling to areas where there is more work is common all over the world. Until

recently in Britain, for example, it was marked by a movement from the north to the south, as people were encouraged to 'Get on your bike'. Huge rural to urban shifts accompany industrialisation, and as areas of wealth and poverty become more concentrated so migration increases.

Demsee's Story

Demsee was taken from her village, Maburka, in Sierra Leone, to the capital, Freetown, when she was about eight years old. Her father received the use of a shack containing two rooms and a 'bathroom' when he handed her over to a Lebanese businessman and his family.[2] Demsee was a domestic worker from the age of nine. Every day began at six o'clock. Apart from being nurse to two young children, she had to give the two schoolboys their breakfast, make sure they had their school uniforms, and keep them clean. She also had to feed the baby. All the house cleaning was her responsibility as well as the skivvying for the gardener, chauffeur, cook, watchman and houseboy. If the washerman failed to come to work, she had to do his job too. The only food she was given were leftovers and dry bread. Physical abuse was a daily constant. 'I was always being beaten. I was beaten so much that after a while I didn't really feel it any more.' Her master raped her from the age of nine onwards, and, when she was ten, he forced her to be circumcised. She put up a fight, but to no avail. 'Finally I was circumcised. Later he said, "Show me".'

Demsee was brought to London by her employers seven or eight times from the age of twelve onwards. The ceaseless work and sexual abuse continued. She was kept isolated, but managed to make friends with a Jamaican woman, Blossom, whom she met in Regent's Park. It was Blossom who convinced her that she should run away. And so started a life on the run, doing illegal cleaning jobs for short periods and staying with unknown people, always on the move in London.

Domestic service is one of the most available of employment opportunities for women migrating from the countryside to the city. In 1986 'Manushi', an Indian women's magazine conducted a survey of Tamil women domestics who had migrated to New Delhi:

> The picture that emerges from the women's accounts of migration is one of human beings shifting for survival. What they hoped to find in this distant city was not a life of luxury but a life that would ensure two meals a day and a life without debts.[3]

The survey found that the women came from the poorest families: agricultural labourers or small farmers, whose holding was so small it could not provide enough food in the year. They were driven from their villages by drought, low wages and underemployment which kept them idle, and consequently indebted for six months of the year. All had to sell or mortgage their land or hut to cover the train fare.

Women had fewer opportunities of urban employment than men and their wages were lower. Since employment was often obtained through friends and contacts it was difficult to break out of a vicious circle, whereby those women already in Delhi worked as domestics, and could therefore only introduce new women migrants into that area of work. Their average income per month was Rs220. This compared with the lowest salary for a male unskilled railway worker of Rs700.

Daughters of domestics tend to follow in their mothers' footsteps. Migrants are even less likely than other poor people to send their children to school. Girls often drop out at an early age to look after younger siblings. By the time a girl is ten she can be earning money independently by cleaning one or two houses, and four years later she is working the same number of employers as an adult woman:

> *But work for the women does not end at 4pm. The women are entirely responsible for the work that needs to be done back home. Lakshmi, 14, returns home at 5pm after finishing the work of her five employers and gets down to the same routine in her own house which she shares with her parents and two younger siblings. She cleans the dishes, fetches water and cleans the dwelling place.*[4]

There is a longing for life in the village and secure land of one's own: 'It would be difficult if one had to wash dishes in Delhi forever. It would be good if we could buy land and run our family in the village'. Younger women and girls long for education and holidays, but acknowledge: 'If I don't work I won't be paid, and if I am not paid I won't be able to eat. Therefore, I must work'.[5]

A domestic servant then has little choice: if her employer tells her that she must come to Britain, come to Britain she must.

Internal migration can be a precursor to international migration. This is particularly true for domestic servants. Women who have travelled some way to enter domestic service are told to accompany their employer when they travel. A large number of Indian domestic workers for example, now enter Britain with Indian employers.

Regional Migration

Although international migration is most commonly thought of as movement from south to north, from the countries of Asia and Africa to Europe and the United States, regional migration is increasingly important.

This can be clearly seen in recent developments in the Asian labour market, hard hit by the decline in the labour demand from the Middle East. Forced to look elsewhere to sell their labour, Asian labour surplus countries found in the newly rich Asian countries an apparent solution: Japan, Taiwan, South Korea, Singapore, and also Malaysia and Thailand, have been increasing their import of labour from the Philippines, Indonesia, Bangladesh, Pakistan and Burma. Some economists believe that the migration patterns developing in Asia are a form of social stratification. Thus Thailand is attracting growing numbers of Burmese to its Northern labour markets, while at the same time, 18 per cent of its migrants are travelling to East Asian countries[6]. Similarly, Malaysia imports hundreds of thousands of workers from Indonesia and the Philippines, but it is also a significant labour exporter to Singapore.

> *Rosenda returned to her home town in Central Luzon, Philippines, after only two months of work as domestic help in Kuala Lumpur. She was in a state of severe depression bordering on psychosis. There was evidence of her being sexually molested by her male employers. In addition, she had lost her sole property, a plot of land, inherited from her parents, where she used to grow vegetables and fruit trees. To raise the agency fee of 15,000 pesos (£323) she had sold the land to the recruiter who had promised a good, lucrative job in Malaysia.*
>
> *Filipina domestics were first noticed in Malaysia in 1986 when 200 of them were deported for having, unknown to themselves, forged documents. They were not compensated for the loss of the fee they had paid the agencies in good faith.*[7]

Regional migration within Asia has been increasing during the 1980s. In 1979 only 9,100 Filipinos were granted tourist visas by the Japanese embassy. In 1986 the figure reached 77,275.[8] In Thailand the number of migrants to East Asia was 7,937 in 1985, and 21,600 in 1988.[9] Although the trade in domestic servants has been going for nearly a decade now, Thailand, India and Bangladesh are increasingly providing maids for Hong Kong and Singapore, whereas before almost all had come from the Philippines.

There are an estimated 66,000 Filipino housemaids in Hong Kong[10] and some 50,000 in Singapore.[11] Both of these destinations are considered preferable to the

ACĒ Int'l Services & Vision Production

For Filipina, Sri-Lankan, Thai maid, houseboys/drivers. Direct, finish, break, terminated/well trained from Philippines/Singapore. Available now. Cheapest yet good service. Door to door services. Open from Mon - Sun & holidays from 9am-9pm

Tel. 8655634, 5286191   Fax. 8655634
Add: 76 Jaffe Rd, 2/F Rm A, Hang Shun Mansion, Wanchai, HK.

Advertisement from the *Hongkong Standard* 5th June 1991

Middle East, perhaps partly because although legislation in both these countries is harsh, there is at least a set of policies and legislation for migrant domestic helpers. This is a significant difference from the United Kingdom.

Migration and Debt

The most common characteristic in Third World migration, whether it be internal or international, is poverty. The majority of migrants are poor. Migration cannot then be said to be a simple matter of choice. Many people migrate simply to survive, to repay personal debts, to provide basic needs for their families, to cover the cost of medical care, or to pay for children's and siblings' education. Since domestic servants are predominantly women, family responsibilities weigh heavy, and unemployment or underemployment at home is often a fact of life. Migration may also mean a level of economic independence not otherwise achievable, and it can bring escape from oppressive personal situations.

Some young women are denied even this narrow choice. It is not uncommon for parents to give their girl child to richer relatives or neighbours in return for assurances that they will provide for her education or medical care. All too often this is not the case. This is not necessarily because of bad will on the part of the employer: migrants settled in Britain may offer a place in their home for a poorer relative in return for child care, and find that there simply is not the time for her to attend college and work. So the young woman spends her time doing menial domestic chores in return for nothing but her keep.

Of course, poverty is not an individual problem, it is also a national disaster. Labour emigration is often encouraged by governments as a partial solution to unemployment which goes some way to alleviate the possibility of social upheaval, often the result of mass unemployment. This is not only through the actual jobs available, but also in the very possibility of overseas work as a potential solution to people's problems.

Above all, however, labour exporters are driven by the need for foreign exchange. In a speech before the First National Congress on Overseas Employment in July 1982, then President Marcos of the Philippines said:

> *For us, overseas employment addresses two major problems: unemployment and the balance of payments position. If these problems are met or at least partially so by contract migration, we also expect an increase in national savings and investment levels.*

In fact, labour export which began as a temporary government policy under Marcos, was expanded under President Aquino, who embarked on an even more aggressive marketing strategy for Filipino labour. Between 1982 and 1985 under Marcos an average of just over 440,500 workers were processed a year. Between 1986 and 1989 this average increased to 637,300.[12] Their remittances were used to help

Jennifer's Story

Jennifer was born in Freetown. Her father died when she was about seven. Her mother survives by growing vegetables in a patch behind her shack and by labouring for her brother at harvest. She had seven children, and after the death of her husband, gave Jennifer to a shopkeeper to take to Beirut, in return for assurances that she would be educated and paid wages every month.

The reality in Beirut was very different. Every day began at 5.30am and frequently ended at 1.30am. The main meal was always at midnight, and there could be any number from 20 to 50 to feed:

> *I was often so tired I fell asleep over my food. I was not allowed to eat until they had finished and then I was only allowed to eat what they left. If I did not work fast enough they shouted at me and called me slave and dog. Always they threatened to kill me if something went wrong.*

She was not allowed to shelter from the bombing of Lebanon's civil war, though during lulls in hostilities she had to visit her employers in their shelter and bring them coffee and food:

> *Sometimes I stood on the balcony when they were firing and thought why not let them kill me? I would be better off dead. This life is not worth living.*

Jennifer was not yet fourteen years old.

The family brought her to London some years later, and she worked in St John's Wood. She was helped to escape by a cleaner, who bundled her out of the house and into a taxi.

alleviate the two major economic problems facing the Aquino government, and which continue to plague the new administration: the rising cost of imports due to the IMF imposed import liberalization plan and the weak Peso combined with the ballooning national debt. Overseas workers thus provide dollars for importers and for paying off the debt. These remittances also benefit approximately 3.2 million Filipinos.[13]

Table 2.1
REMITTANCES, EXPORTS, IMPORTS AND EXTERNAL DEBT 1986-1988. (US$ MILLION)

	1986	1987	1988
Remittances (R)*	695.56	808.81	856.81
Exports (X)	4842	5720	7074
Imports (Y)	5044	6737	8159
Foreign Debt(D)	2937	3005	2983
R/X	14.36%	14.14%	12.11%
R/Y	13.79%	12.05%	10.50%
R/D	23.68%	26.92%	28.72%

* Official Central Bank figures.
Source: Philippine Migration Review Vol.1V No.2

As in many Third World countries the Philippine debt problem began in the 1970s with the oil price hikes that were to bring so much wealth to the Middle East. At the same time as poor countries were experiencing increased balance of payments deficits, due partly to the rising price of oil imports, banks in the First World were overflowing with 'petrodollars', the new millions deposited by the Middle East nations. The solution? To lend money to Third World countries, who were given every encouragement to borrow. In 1965, the Philippines' foreign debt was some US$600 million. This trebled in five years to $2.297 billion. In 1987, the country's debt reached $28,566 million, a per capita burden of $502 for a country whose per capita GNP was only $500.[14]

In the 1980s as the world economy contracted, interest rates soared. The Philippines like so many other countries, is caught in a debt trap, having to borrow to pay its interest thereby increasing its debt. Between 1987 and 1992, it is estimated that the Philippines paid an average of $2.3 billion interest and $1.3 billion principal a year.[15]

There are now between 3 and 3.5 million overseas Filipinos in over 120 different countries. At least one million of them are women, working mainly as domestics. The aggregate cash and merchandise remittances of Filipino migrants for 1989 are estimated to be somewhere between US$2 to $3 billion.[16] Remittances from migrants constituted the country's number one source of foreign exchange between 1986 and 1988, even according to notoriously unreliable figures of the Central Bank. (Unreliable because it is common knowledge that the majority of Filipinos prefer to use 'unofficial channels', like returning friends or money couriers, rather than banks, in the returning of remittances.)

Nor is this situation peculiar to the Philippines. In Sri Lanka remittances are surpassed only by tea exports as the country's principal foreign exchange earner. As in the Philippines, the foreign exchange is vital for the government's economic policies, for offsetting part of its balance of payments deficit and for paying for imports.

If Third World debt is considered a form of debt bondage, then the indebted countries may be considered to be nations in servitude to the rich North. Instead of producing the basic commodities needed so desperately by their people, the economy is geared towards export to earn foreign exchange to be used to pay off the debt. This is clearly seen in the labour market: throughout the Third World there is a desperate need for skilled people, not just teachers, doctors and nurses, but workers to build up infrastructure, roads, bridges, piped water, sewage, electrification etc. Labour export is draining countries of their skilled human resource base. Moreover, those workers are being trained, 'produced' and paid for at home; it is their own country and compatriots, not the rich North, that is paying for them when they are unproductive, while they are young, or when they have been forced to return home because they are too old to work. By the time they have returned, migrants have usually become deskilled, they have not been able to use their original training, and it is often even harder for them to find employment.

Migrants' remittances do not provide a long term solution to economic problems. Money is not invested in ways which increase the country's capital stock, it is spent on paying off debts, on food, medical care and education. Consumer goods sold in these countries, such as radios, washing machines, televisions, are manufactured elsewhere, and the migrants' hard earned money is ploughed indirectly into other economies. Any improvement in lifestyle is not to be sneered at, but while the houses built from the wages of overseas domestics may be built of solid concrete, like their poorer neighbours' they have no piped water, no road to their door and no electricity.

The women themselves are also often caught in a vicious cycle of debt which ties them to their employer. Middle East Watch found many cases in Kuwait where women's salaries had been withheld by employers, allegedly to settle their debts. In most cases, employment agents had charged the employer a commission and the cost of the domestic's airfare, telling the employers to recoup the money from the maids. The domestics have usually already paid duplicate fees to the agents, and so find themselves doubly indebted.

> *The women workers appeared to have no say in the amount attributed as loaned to them or in the decision regarding salary proportions to be deducted towards their debt. In many cases we investigated, debt had the effect of placing women in bondage to their employers. It was used as a means of forcing the women to endure prolonged working hours, inadequate food and sleep, no days off, and no time to attend a place of worship, for fear of never getting paid or of losing their jobs.*[17]

Migration is an expensive business, and often requires the mortgaging of land for instance, or borrowing a large sum of money. If remittances are not enough to keep up payment, land is lost and families are forced to work as farm labourers, the poorest of the poor. Thus the migrant is burdened with a large personal debt to repay as well as the knowledge that their family is dependent on them for their earnings.

Recruitment agencies also act as loan sharks, advancing loans to enable women to pay their fees, with interest as high as 50 per cent. Recruitment agencies for Filipino domestics in Hong Kong have a particularly bad reputation for this. They often demand passports as collateral for loans of HK$10,000 (£687). When the woman needs to renew her visa she must either borrow from other sources to retrieve her passport, or pay a fee to the agency for 'borrowing' her own property, or simply not renew her visa, and risk deportation or imprisonment. It has been estimated that up to 70 per cent of Filipina domestics have taken a loan while in Hong Kong, and it is generally thought that as many as 50 per cent are in serious debt.[18] There is a tendency for employers, when they discover their domestic is heavily in debt to summarily dismiss her. Some agencies capitalise on this and threaten disclosure as a means of debt recovery.

Recruitment Processes

As we have seen, labour migration is not simply a matter of individual 'choice'. The governments of receiving and sending countries 'pull' and 'push' respectively while encouraging and controlling the migration of labour as it suits their needs.

In Sri Lanka, for example, the government, alarmed by the 'brain drain' and its consequences, positively discouraged international migration until 1977 when circumstances changed dramatically. The United National Party (UNP) won a landslide victory and liberalisation of the economy brought a drop in living standards and a decrease in real wages. The UNP encouraged migration at the same time as poverty increased, and modern consumer goods flooded the market. It established foreign missions, subsidised migrants' airfares to the Middle East, and liberalised the export of foreign currency. It even granted those in government service two years' leave for foreign employment. In general however, migrants tend to be from lower income groups, and to travel to the Middle East. Seventy per cent of Sri Lankan migrants to the Middle East are women, and the vast majority of them are domestic workers.

The reliance of the Sri Lankan economy on female wage work is by no means a recent phenomenon. Women provided the majority of labour in the plantations, and after independence continued their contribution not only in the plantations but also in agriculture, in textile and food manufacturing, and in the informal sector. They were particularly hard hit by the economic restructuring after 1977:

> *Not only do they (the poorest households) typically lack productive assets, and depend for livelihoods on unskilled labour, but they tend to be disproportionately dependent on the earnings of unskilled female labour. In the worst cases they are women with dependent children but no access to adult male earnings, their husbands having died, deserted or become unable to work. These are the women who depend above all on a regular job plucking tea or tapping rubber. And these are the people upon whom the.....strategies of all Sri Lankan governments have borne most heavily.* [19]

The Sri Lankan migrant to the Middle East is typically female and married with young children.

It is widely acknowledged, however, that it is not the sending country that determines the numbers and profile of its migrants, but the labour importer. So the question remains, why is it that such a large proportion of Sri Lankan migrants to the Middle East are women? One important factor is that Sri Lanka was relatively late in joining the exodus to the Middle East. By the time it came on to the scene, recruitment of domestics had been banned by Pakistan and Bangladesh, and restricted by India because of complaints of abuse and exploitation. Sri Lankan women then, filled this gap. This has meant that, while migration from many other Asian countries has declined since 1982 and the end of the Middle East construction boom, migration from Sri Lanka has remained stable. It has also meant that Sri Lankans have featured prominently in cases of ill-treatment and abuse. The Sri Lanka mission in Saudi Arabia was established in November 1981, and almost immediately reported that it had received 200 complaints, mainly from domestics, including torture, assault, and sexual harassment.

There are four main means of recruitment to the Middle East: through the Bureau of Foreign Employment (BFE); authorised recruitment agencies; unauthorised agents; friends and relatives in the Middle East. Those who have worked there before can also have direct contact with previous employers.

The BFE was established in 1985 to monitor recruiting agencies, to promote employment opportunities overseas and to protect the rights of migrants. It also serves as an employment intermediary.

This involvement of the government in the actual recruiting of migrants is not peculiar to Sri Lanka. Indeed in the Philippines the wholesale involvement of the government was one of the main reasons for the popularity of Filipino migrant labour. This was partly because labour export was taken on so wholeheartedly by the government, who provided publicity, infrastructure and organisation, thereby making the Filipino migrant very easily obtainable for an employer. It was also because of the continuing squeeze on the middle classes, which has resulted in large numbers of well-educated, English-speaking unemployed. Even in work where these qualifications apparently have little relevance – and domestic work would be one of those areas – the worker with academic qualifications has the competitive edge.

In the early 70s Marcos created the Overseas Employment Development Board (OEDB) to facilitate and control the export of labour. It was intended that the government should have full control and responsibility for recruitment, and in 1974 it announced that private recruiters and agencies would be phased out and be replaced by the OEDB. However, the OEDB simply could not cope with the numbers of workers it was having to process, and from 1978 private recruitment was positively encouraged.

In 1982 President Marcos created a single body to deal with all matters relating to labour migration, the Philippine Overseas Employment Administration (POEA). Its brief was:

> *The promotion and development of employment opportunities abroad... in cooperation with relevant government agencies and entities as well as representative groups from the private sector, through organised market promotion activities and services which shall include among others, the following:*

a) a comprehensive manpower marketing strategy and despatch of marketing missions abroad for this purpose;

b) to develop and promote programs or arrangements that would encourage the hiring of Filipinos in organised or corporate groups as well as government to government arrangements;

c) to promote Filipino manpower through advertising in appropriate media overseas.[20]

POEA offices are always crowded and 'facilitators', those who know individual civil servants and how to play the system, can therefore cut down on the waiting time – often several months. They are, however, only available for a fee. There are allegations of larger scale corruption: in the summer of 1990, the POEA administrator resigned after severe criticism and accusations of mismanagement, corruption and nepotism. He was replaced by Jose Sarmiento, administrator of the Overseas Workers' Welfare Administration (OWAA), who had himself been investigated for alleged misuse of funds and had been involved in several scandals,

Advertisement from the *Philippine Daily Inquirer* 3rd June 1991

Two leading reputable agencies in HK

announce more openings for

116 DOMESTIC HELPERS

for gainful deployment in Hongkong to earn HK$3,000/mo. plus other benefits and the golden chance to work in Canada after contract. HK Principal interview on:

BEXLEY INT'L. LTD. -- June 4 & July 2
   Acc. # 25481-5

TOP SERVICES & CO. -- June 11 & July 9
   Acc. # 24477-4

Req: Police Clearance, ID Photo, Birth and Marriage Certificates, Employment Cert. (if possible) & Diploma.
At least high school graduate, 21-38 years old, can speak English, hardworking and responsible.

You can trust us.
"HONGKONG PLACEMENT IS OUR EXPERTISE"

DESERTWEALTH Int'l Services Corp.

(POEA) Lic. No. 03-0738
2nd Floor, Oandasan Bldg.
507 Malvar St. cor. Mabini, Malate, Manila
Near Pistang Pilipino
THIS AD IS APPROVED BY POEA

including in 1989 the stranding of 300 Filipinas in Beirut, who were forced to turn to prostitution in order to survive, while the Philippines' authorities wrangled over whose responsibility they were.

If the public sector is riddled with corruption, the private sector is characterised by deceit, cheating, over-charging and false promises. In Sri Lanka as in the Philippines the private sector deal with the bulk of migrants. The number of people who use the BFE is small and progressively decreasing. It is far more common for workers to go through the private sector or informally through personal contacts. Many of the private agencies are unregistered. A registered agency must pay Rs 10,000 (£121) for their licence, and Rs 100,000 (£1210) bank guarantee. There is a maximum commission chargeable per migrant of Rs 2,700 (£32), and the agent has to send in a monthly report to the BFE to assist its data gathering. Fraud is common: it is not unusual for agents to disappear as soon as the migrant pays their fee. Agents collect passports and advance fee as soon as they promise a job. Even if they do return the fee if they fail to find a post, the worker in the meantime will have been paying an extortionate monthly interest.

Domestics are often recruited by sub-agents who tour the villages on the agencies' behalf. This is open to great abuse since sub-agents frequently receive no payment from the agent, but must extract it from the worker. Similarly agents, who used to receive a commission from their counterpart in the Middle East, now have to pay to place workers, and this is reflected in their fees.

Recruitment fees have soared. In 1980 64 per cent of migrants left Sri Lanka without having to pay fees. By 1985 this had dropped to 45 per cent. Agencies, legal or illegal, rarely charge the legal fee, and Rs 15,000 (£181) is not unusual. There are still plenty of places for domestics, and their recruitment cost is relatively low, yet still it has rocketed. In the early 80s it was Rs 826 (£10), but by 1986 it had increased to Rs 4,314 (£52). Because they come from poor families, some 60 per cent of domestics have to borrow, mortgage or pawn to cover their recruitment costs[21]. This can cause tremendous difficulties: even if they have a bona fide recruiter, exorbitant interest rates translate into several months' labour in the Middle East, and disaster if the person has to return home early.

In 1983 the POEA formally permitted private recruiting agencies to charge fees, placing a ceiling of 5,000 pesos (£107) to cover passport, insurance, inoculation, medical examinations, travel taxes etc. In reality, agencies charge far more, and take the opportunity for a multitude of duplicitous practices: workers may be asked to pay for air fares which have already been covered by the employer; they offer ten jobs to one hundred applicants; send migrants to fictitious work sites and dump them in another part of the Philippines. Agents go from door to door in villages and small towns promising prosperity to those who will take the chance: 'Your friend and your companion in each step you take', they promise. They take an advance and run, or charge astronomical fees: 20,000 pesos (£431) for jobs in the

Middle East, 40,000 pesos (£863) for those in Hong Kong, and 60,000 pesos (£1290) for work in Western Europe.

The excesses of the private recruitment sector have long been known. As early as 1979 the government formed its own Task Force on Illegal Recruitment, and in 1983 DOLE said 50 per cent of irregularities reported to it were perpetrated by legal agencies. The abuse was so flagrant in the case of domestic workers that in May 1991 the POEA stated that it would set up a household workers' placement unit and handle all applications for domestic work in Hong Kong. Private agencies would no longer be allowed to operate in this field. Workers in future may have to pay only 1,920 pesos (£41) for their passport and other documents. In announcing the changes the POEA admitted that some applicants had had to pay as much as 30,000 pesos (£647). The move was generally welcomed by concerned groups with the rider that overseeing of all transactions was vital, otherwise new opportunities for corruption would have been created within the POEA.

1 See Busia, Nana "Domestic Servants in Ghana" 1992 in *The Reporter*, 13 (8), Anti-Slavery International, for a discussion of the abuse of workers which can stem from such ahistorical relationships.
2 Sierra Leone has a large Lebanese trading community.
3 Prabha, Rani, and Poonam, Kaul 1986. "For Two Meals a Day: A Report on Tamil Domestic Maids", *Manushi* no.35, 6(5), New Delhi: Manushi Trust.
4 Manushi, ibid.
5 Manushi, ibid.
6 *Far Eastern Economic Review*, 2nd April 1992, p.20.
7 "Women and International Migration". Meeting held in Quezon City, December 1987.
8 *The Trade in Domestic Helpers: Causes, Mechanisms and Consequences*. 1989, Asian and Pacific Development Centre, p.140.
9 *The Labour Trade: Filipino Migrant Workers throughout the World*, 1987. London: Catholic Institute for International Relations.
10 *Asian Migrant Forum*, 1991-1992, Issues 3 & 4. (see Chapter 6 note 2).
11 ASI: unpublished research.
12 "Overview on Filipino Labour-Outmigration" *Philippine Migration Review*, 4 (3), fourth quarter 1990.
13 1985 Family Income and Expenditures Survey of the Philippine National Census and Statistics Office. Quoted in *Philippine Migration Review*, ibid.
14 "It's a Debtly Affair!". *Philippine Migration Review* 4 (2), third quarter 1990, p.17.
15 Serrano, I. Unpublished mss. Philippine Rural Reconstruction Movement, Manila.
16 "Overseas Workers' Remittances and the Philippine Debt Problem" *Philippine Migration Review*, 4 (3), third quarter 1990, p.4.
17 "Punishing the Victim: Rape and Mistreatment of Asian Maids in Kuwait", 1992. *Middle East Watch: Women's Rights Project* 4 (8), New York and Washington: Human Rights Watch.
18 ASI: unpublished research.
19 Manor James ed 1984. *Sri Lanka in Change and Crisis*, Chapter 7, London and Sydney: Croom Helm.
20 National Economic and Development Authority, Philippine Development Plan 1978-1982.
21 Figures on Sri Lankan agency fees from Eelens F. and Speckmann, J. "Recruitment of Labour Migrants for the Middle East" in Eelens, Schampers and Speckmann eds, 1992. *Labour Migration to the Middle East: from Sri Lanka to the Gulf*, London: Kegan Paul International.

CHAPTER THREE

Mama's a Maid in London
Domestic Slavery in the United Kingdom

When I came to London I thought freedom was here at last. I really didn't think I would meet all these problems. I thought I would be able to choose whatever job I wanted like the rest of the legal Filipinos here. I didn't know what life is like for a Filipina who, like in my case, had run away from her employer. When my companion said to me, 'From now on you must beware of the Home Office', I said, 'What is Home Office?' I didn't know anything about it. She said to me, 'Oh, you must be careful. After your visa expires you will become an illegal immigrant here.' I said, 'Why can't I get a job and then they will give me a work permit?' She told me that this wasn't possible, there were no work permits now. I said, 'God, I didn't know there would be all these problems for me.' But it was already too late.

Having left their homes in order to enable themselves and their families to survive, women like Alice often do not realise the odds are stacked against them when they become migrant workers.

So many women have gone abroad to work as domestics, that the phenomenon has entered popular culture. At the end of the 1980s a Filipino pop group, Smokey Mountain, had a success with a song called Mama, the refrain of which is:

> *Mama's a maid in London*
> *I want to believe that she's fine*
> *She could be lonely in London*
> *I want to know why she had to go*
> *I need her*
> *I want to be near her*
> *I've got to be with her*
> *And see to it*
> *That we're together once more.*

The abuse which many domestic servants endure is not restricted to the Middle East. It also takes place in London, behind the well polished doors of Hampstead, Knightsbridge and Chelsea, where it is meted out by wealthy employers of many nationalities, British, Indian, Nigerian, Kuwaiti, Cypriot, to name but a few. The domestics come from a range of Third World countries, including Sri Lanka, India, Nigeria, Sierra Leone and Morocco. The largest recorded number, however, come from the Philippines via the Gulf States. Although most domestics working in the Gulf States are Sri Lankan, it is the Filipinas who are employed by the wealthiest employers who are the most likely to travel.

There are two identified 'routes' through which private domestics commonly enter the UK: directly from their country of origin, or via a second country, with employers from that country, usually the Middle East, but also Hong Kong and Singapore. Whatever the route, they do not enter Britain because they choose to do so but because they have to.

Efforts to establish the numbers of overseas domestic workers entering the United Kingdom each year have been frustrated by the fact that government offices have not been able to supply reliable figures. Neither the Home Office nor the Department of Employment were able to satisfy Mr Peter Archer's questions on this matter asked in the House of Commons in November and December of 1990, maintaining that the information was not available[1]. It was not until 1992 that any official figures were mentioned, when the Foreign Office stated that between January and August only 439 'concessionary visas' were issued.[2] However, Kalayaan, a support organisation working with and for migrant domestic workers, disputes this number as grossly inaccurate. Their research shows that during the same period 247 domestic workers sought help after having fled abusive employers. Calculating from information received from these workers who have left their employers, together with the knowledge that many workers continue to stay with their employers, it is safe to assume the number to be much higher. As a result of research and documentation carried out by Kalayaan and the Commission For Filipino Migrant Workers (CFMW), they estimated that there are some 4,500 abused domestics in Britain. This estimate, was arrived at by extrapolating from the 1,600 workers known to CFMW by 1992/93. But each of those women knows of one, sometimes two or three other women incarcerated and exploited as they had been. Moreover, instances have recently come to light of young Latin American and African women in similar circumstances, but outside the Philippines – Middle East – Britain circuit, and therefore unknown to domestics involved in the research. There is at present no way of estimating their numbers.

There are several thousand foreign private resident domestics workers in Britain, and they continue to enter the country, yet there is no provision for the admission of private domestic servants under British immigration law. This means that it is very difficult, not to say impossible, for workers to have access to the legal protection that theoretically they have a right to.

Resident Domestics – 'Here to do certain jobs'

From the late 1960s Commonwealth immigration was severely restricted, yet there

> ## Roseline's Story
>
> Roseline is from Southern Nigeria. At the age of about 15 she was 'bought' for £2 from her impoverished father who was led to believe he would be paid that sum regularly every month to help feed his other five children. Roseline, he was told by the couple, was to stay as their guest and be taught domestic science. They brought her to Sheffield, where the husband worked as a doctor. She was kept as a servant, not allowed out, slept on the floor and was made to kneel on the floor for two hours if she fell asleep before being allowed to go to bed. Her working day started at 5.30am and lasted for 18 hours. She cleaned and washed for her employers and their five children. She was caned and kept short of food. On one occasion, in desperation, she wrote a note intended for the next door neighbour offering sex for a sandwich. The note was discovered and she was further punished. In September 1988, while her abusers were away for a week, she gathered enough courage and spoke to a regular passer-by who had often seen her staring out of the window, and beckoned to her. This neighbour helped her to escape, and she took her former employers to court. She was awarded £20,000 in damages. However, she had only been given leave to stay for three months, and her employers had kept her for over three years. She was an illegal overstayer and thus liable to immediate deportation.

was a continuing need for cheap labour. Clothing manufacturers, the National Health Service and the hotel and catering industries in particular were forced to look elsewhere and new countries began to figure in the immigration statistics – Southern Europe, Colombia, Turkey and the Philippines. Between 1973 and 1976, 7,278 work permits were issued to people from the Philippines, as opposed to 1,772 to people from India, one of Britain's traditional sources of cheap labour.[3]

During this period most non-Commonwealth resident private domestics came to Britain under the work permit system. This was a similar system to that currently employed in the Gulf States, whereby the work permit was issued, not to the worker, but to the employer, who had to prove to the Department of Employment that the worker was suitable for a particular post, and that there was no one else in Britain who could do that work. The work permit had to be renewed annually by the same employer making it virtually impossible for the worker to complain of bad conditions, non-payment of wages etc. Although outside the written rules, in practice, if a worker found another employer willing to offer a job in the same category of work, a new permit could be applied for by the new employer enabling the worker to change employers. For four years the worker could not change employment category. However at the end of that period she could settle permanently and be joined by her family, as well as having the new freedom to change employment category.

Work permits were a means of tying the worker as closely as possible to the needs of the British economy. Thus in 1971 when it was announced that work permits for men would only be available for skilled work, an exception was made for the hotel and catering industry where special quotas were allowed for unskilled and semi-skilled work. The reasons for this exception were rendered quite explicit by Mr Dudley Smith, then Under-Secretary in the Department of Employment:

> *There was considerable pressure on the Department from hoteliers and from people in the catering industry crying out for people to be imported to do certain jobs, largely because they could not get white people to do them. All right, I accept the responsibility, because my party was in government at the time, that inevitably, although not on a wholesale scale, the Department and the Government gave way on this and allowed a certain number to come in, and that position remains today.*[4]

The new restrictions on the work permit system were instituted under the Immigration Rules. These set out the administration of the Immigration Act. The Rules regulate the entry and stay of visitors, students, workers, and dependants, none of whom are covered by the Act itself. They also detail the 'general considerations' which should be borne in mind by immigration officers in their work. The Rules are of vital importance, but they are what is known as secondary legislation. This means law which is made by the Secretary of State and simply presented to Parliament where it can only be voted on in its entirety with no opportunity for amendments. This differs from primary legislation (ie an act of Parliament) which has to go through committee stages and readings in both Houses.

In February 1975 the restriction on work permits was extended to unskilled women, but again an exception was made, this time for resident domestic workers. That year 66 per cent of permits issued to resident domestics were issued to Filipinos. Other communities represented included Latin American, Moroccan, Portuguese and Turkish. It was under this and the hotel and catering categories that the majority of the Filipino community came to Britain. They were restricted to menial jobs. About half the Filipinas were employed in hospitals and nursing homes, and the other 50 per cent was split between maids in private houses, and restaurant and hotel workers.

The quotas were progressively reduced: as from August 1977 only European women were permitted to enter Britain as domestic workers. At the end of 1979, quotas were phased out altogether. By this time there were no longer any non-European resident domestic workers entering the country.

Work permits are now only available, either to employees at board level earning £50,000 or more, or for work which cannot be done by a United Kingdom or European Community national. Work permit holders may still change jobs within the same category of employment as before, providing the new employer first obtains a work permit, and after four years of working the work permit holder has a right to settle. Work permits are now usually given only for highly skilled and professional jobs.

The 'Concession'

So, since 1977 it has not been possible for non-Europeans to enter this country as foreign resident domestics, and yet the process undoubtedly continues. Given the stringent immigration control at ports of entry, how is this possible?

Wealthy individuals and returning British nationals are allowed to bring in their domestic servants under a special concession. Under this concession until 1991 the employer could bring in their domestics under one of two categories, as 'visitors' or as 'persons named to work with a specified employer'. Immigration officials were issued with the following guidelines 'In Confidence':

> *A person engaged abroad as a domestic servant, who has been in the service of the employer for more than twelve months abroad may accompany the employer to the United Kingdom to continue the employment. The employer must undertake to provide maintenance and accommodation for any dependants and the Immigration Officer must be satisfied that the person intends to continue in the employment. Domestics may be allowed to benefit from this arrangement even if they are outside the normal age limits or have dependent children. Leave to enter should be given on Code 4 for up to twelve months. (Code 4 gives leave to enter on condition that the holder only engages in employment for a particular named person; the holder is required to register with the police.)*

> *Domestic servants, chauffeurs, private secretaries and other employees who render personal service may be allowed to enter with their employers if only a visit is intended in which case leave to enter as a visitor on Code 3 for the period of the employer's authorised stay is appropriate. (Code 3 gives leave to enter for a specified period on condition that the holder does not enter employment paid or unpaid; again, the holder has to register with the police.) If the employer is to remain in the United Kingdom other than as a visitor eg for settlement or to set up in business, such employees require work permits.*

In practice, since there are no clear guidelines for immigration officials, the stamp given is often a matter of chance, and in fact many domestics are given a stamp under Code 5N, simply, 'Leave to enter, employment prohibited'.

Domestic workers are, therefore, not given an immigration status independent of the household they work for. As the then Home Office Minister, David Waddington stated in a letter to Lord Avebury:

> *Admission in such cases is on the basis that the employee will be expected to*

leave the country with the employer, or on prior termination of the employment. [5]

They are treated as members of the household, and their status as employee is unrecognised. As in the Gulf States where labour laws do not recognise domestics as workers, but treat them as household members, this non-recognition renders them liable to abuse. Importantly, although applications for extensions to remain with the original employers are usually granted, applications to change employers are routinely refused on the basis that no work permit was held on entry.

In 1991, after several years of campaigning by the workers themselves and by their support group, Kalayaan, the Home Office announced that as a means of protecting workers from abuse and exploitation they were going to require that the entry clearance officer screen the incoming domestic worker more carefully, to check the bona fides of the domestic arrangement. The official would check that the worker had been employed by the employer for a minimum of twelve months overseas already, and was at least 17 years old. This information would be gathered and confirmed through an interview with the worker before leaving her country of residence. She and her employer would also be issued with a pamphlet detailing the legal rights and protection for domestic workers.

These kinds of restrictions have in fact been imposed on migrant communities before, again because of reports of abuse. In 1973 the entry of unskilled Filipinos under the work permit system was halted as a direct response to the 'Rochdale Case'. Alderglen, a clothing manufacturer, had recruited Filipino women through advertisements in Manila offering £40 a week, not mentioning that this was the top rate, available only to skilled machinists. The majority of women found that they earned a basic pay of £12, minus £1 to repay their air fare. They lived in overcrowded accommodation with inadequate facilities.

The adverse publicity was countered by a temporary ban on unskilled Filipino workers until 'safeguards' for their employment could be instituted. Two years later these were finally given as:

1. that the woman had to be over 20 years old; and
2. that she had to have worked in a similar job abroad for at least one year.

The temporary ban was lifted in February 1975, at the same time as the permanent ban on female unskilled labour apart from resident domestics was announced.

Continuing Abuse

The changes announced by the Home Office in no way address the basic problem. While acknowledging that the women are entering the country as employees, the government is not giving them a status that recognizes that they are workers nor the right to change employers. As the Joint Council for the Welfare of Immigrants have pointed out:

We came across a copy of secret instructions[6] *some years back which state that servants of families should be allowed in with them when they're coming as visitors, even though it's quite clear to the immigration officer and to the family and to everyone that the person is coming to work rather than coming on holiday.*[7]

The government maintains that this concession benefits workers who would otherwise lose their jobs when their employers came to stay in Britain. This seems unlikely: most employers visiting this country have many more domestic servants than those they bring with them, and those who do not accompany them remain in their old posts until their employers return. If it benefited domestic workers it would be strangely perverse for so many of them to campaign for a change in the concession.

However the government also admits that the concession benefits Britain; Lord Reay, speaking for the government, said in 1990:

Looking at our national interest, if wealthy investors, skilled workers and others with the potential to benefit our economy were unable to be accompanied by their domestic staff they might not come here at all but take their money and skills to other countries only too keen to welcome them.[8]

By their actions, the Home Office are denying the women their most basic rights, not only as workers, but also as human beings, for because of these practices employers continue to exercise complete control over their employee. In both entrance categories the domestic cannot legally change employer, whatever the abuse she is subjected to.

The abuse and exploitation that this can lead to is well illustrated by the case of Mrs Laxmi Swami.

Born in India, Laxmi Swami came to Britain via Kuwait under the Home Office Concession as the servant to two half-sisters of the Emir. The princesses regularly spent six months of the year in Bayswater, central London, taking their servants with them. They subjected these women to extreme cruelty, both physical and mental: beatings whether with a broomstick, a knotted electric flex or a horsewhip, were routine; Laxmi's eyes were damaged when they threw a bunch of keys at her face; they yanked out two gold teeth. They told her that one of her four children had been killed in a motorcycle accident, and beat her when she broke down and cried. It was only years later that she discovered they had been lying.

While in London the princesses frequently went out at 8pm and returned home at two or three o'clock in the morning. While they were away Mrs Swami had to stand by the door exactly where they had left her. On their return she had to massage their hands and feet and, should they be in a bad mood, suffer kicks while she did so. She slept, rarely for more than two hours a night, on the floor outside the locked kitchen, drinking forbidden water from the bath tap. She was permanently hungry and often denied food altogether for days at a time. There was plenty of food, but it was in the dustbin and deliberately spoiled so that she could not eat it even if she managed to put her hands between the bars on the windows and reach it.

The windows had been barred after an incident in 1981 when the princesses tried to strangle Laxmi with some electric flex. By chance the front door had not been locked as usual and Mrs Swami, bleeding, managed to run out to the street, and hail a taxi to take her to the Indian High Commission. The officials there sent her back to her abusers because she could not afford the airfare home.

Mrs Laxmi Swami's life in Bayswater is not an isolated case. Lulu's employer had been serving with the British forces in Brunei and had employed Lulu there before bringing her to Britain.

Lulu's Story

I received a very low wage which I accepted because there was no alternative. My employer did not follow the contract. There was no day off. I was maltreated, overworked and few hours sleep. When I arrived in London my employer was always shouting at me for whatever little mistakes I did in the housework. Whenever I said that I was not feeling well my employer would shout back at me: 'Why are you not feeling well? I did not pay for you in the agency to be sick. I paid for you to work'... I wasn't feeling well because the food that I was eating was not enough to sustain me to all of my work. In the morning I would eat a slice of bread and have a cup of tea. During lunch I would usually have a bowl of rice and some water, and in the evening I would have a slice of bread and a cup of tea again... The lady wants me to sleep in the garage if there is a carpet but I argue with her that the garage is only for the car and it's very cold. I told her that I cannot bear to sleep there.

Domestics are particularly vulnerable to rape and sexual abuse. There are cases where this has occurred, not just once, but many, many times. Physical abuse and sexual harassment are only the most extreme of a range of inhuman treatment endured by foreign domestics. Other circumstances may be less sensational, but they are the harsh and dehumanising facts of their lives: they are deprived of contact with their family and access to compatriots and friends; forced to work excessive hours, for low wages – if indeed wages are paid at all; deprived of food and privacy; their contract may be changed or ignored, and their passport confiscated by their employer.

Using all her savings to pay the recruitment agency's fee of 15,000 pesos (£324), Bing, a Filipina domestic worker, travelled to Qatar in the Middle East where she was obliged to sign a contract for considerably less money than originally promised.

> ## Bing's Story
>
> In Qatar she (her employer) paid me every month but when we came to London she never gave me my salary. Even after seven months. She thought that if she paid me what she owed me I would run away. It was very bad because I couldn't send money to my family in all that time. When I finally ran away she still owed me everything and I had to leave behind even my clothes. I had no day off, I was not allowed to go out alone. She didn't shout at me or mistreat me so much here because she felt that this is not her country, she can't do such things here. That is why she used the salary to keep me with her. But in the end I had to leave because my children were suffering because I couldn't send money home.

When her employer left for London she felt she had no option but to follow. As the Earl of Longford has said:

> *There is no doubt that slavery is taking place in England. Who would have thought that such a state of affairs was possible?*

He was speaking in a debate in the House of Lords on 28th November 1990. In the same debate he gave an example of a domestic worker who was not allowed out of her employers' house, was given only scraps to eat, and hit with ashtrays when she displeased them. When she tripped while carrying their child, the mother, an Englishwoman, attacked her with a knife, and was only pulled off by guests, who happened to be in the house.[9]

Such living and working conditions bear a startling resemblance to those which have incurred such criticism in the Gulf. They are not denied by the British authorities who recognise and 'regret' such cases. The Home Office is perfectly aware of the problems faced by domestic servants, as indeed are immigration officials. In the words of one woman:

> *We were two Filipinas coming together to England at the airport with our employer, 'Why do you bring two Filipinas? do you not think that they will run away from you here?' But my employer said, 'I trust them because I've brought them to England twice already'.*

She was admitted as a tourist with no further questions or difficulties.

Legally Condoning Slavery

It is important to point out that this is not a question of 'bad' employers who import slavery, but the structural condoning of such practices through the immigration law and rules. It is not therefore only foreign employers who abuse their employees, and the issue cannot be tackled as such. Because of their manner of entry into the country, these women tend to be employed to a larger degree by non-British nationals, but it is the conditions of entry that must change if they are to be able to rely on the protection of the law.

Cases of abuse have been brought to the attention of the House of Commons, the House of Lords, and the Department of Employment. The latter has in the past held that domestics who are abused should have recourse to industrial tribunals and civil and criminal litigation. Occasionally employers are taken to court, but this is very rare, for, as Lord Hylton has pointed out, the Department of Employment's stand is:

> *totally unrealistic. Few resident domestics will dare to use those procedures while they are still in employment. If they leave or are sacked, they immediately breach their conditions of entry and become liable to deportation. Again, in that situation few will risk embarking on proceedings for which legal aid may not be readily available. Rights are a pure illusion unless they can in practice be fully exercised.*[10]

No Escape

Life in Britain for foreign domestic workers can be unbearable. Running away, which requires tremendous courage, is often the only solution that many abused domestics have. Their employers recognise this, and frequently threaten their workers with the dire consequences of such action; one worker was told:

> *I will cut your face. I will kill you and scatter your pieces in the desert if you ever disobey an order. You are my slave. You will do exactly what I say; eat only when I tell you and only what I give you. If you attempt to steal food, you will be starved until I decide you have learned your lesson. You will sleep on the floor outside my bedroom and only for the hours I tell you. You will have no days off and you will not leave this house unaccompanied. Remember, I hold your passport. If the police find you, you will be deported to where you came from. And, if you are, you will be killed – if I do not manage to kill you first. Don't forget – there are plenty more where you came from.*

Escape is not easy: there are practical difficulties, doors are kept bolted, windows locked and there may be security guards or dogs patrolling the premises; many women have also not been allowed out of the house, so they have no idea where they are, where to go, or how to get there; they have no money, no papers, no friends, no belongings. It is a leap into the unknown, and always there is the fear of their employers discovering them.

Alice came to London after two and a half years in Kuwait to accompany her employers on their annual holiday. She was the only servant of the 56 to come with them, and found that, even more than before, she was worked off her feet. Then, at four o'clock one morning, her male employer called her to make breakfast

Trapped

When you run away from an employer you have no money, no job. The first thing you have to do is find a job but then you get trapped in doing that job. You don't have time to find out how to sort out your situation. If you meet another Filipino, say one who is here legally, and you ask for information or advice about your situation, they tell you 'Just keep quiet. Don't ask too many questions, just work, work.' Because we are afraid we don't get proper advice and information about our status here from those who know what is going on.

for him. He followed her into the kitchen, tore off her clothes, and attempted to rape her. Alice fought back:

> I do not know how, but I managed to kick him there, and he crawled back into his bedroom. But I was so frightened, because he said he would kill me, and I didn't know what he would do. They had a housekeeper there, an Indian woman, and she told me I should run away straight, and go to a church to ask them what to do. She gave me £50 and she helped me to escape, because all the doors were alarmed. So I escaped through the hole in the wall where the pipe from the tumble drier goes. I was very thin then because I did not have enough to eat.

It was Alice's first time to be outside of the house in London. Distraught and barefoot she flagged down a taxi:

> First the taxi driver asked me, 'Do you have any money?', so I gave him the £50. Then he said, 'Where do you want to go?', and I said, in my crooked English, 'The nearest church', 'What kind of church?', 'Catholic'. But he did not take me there, because we were in Hampstead, and he drove me down to Wandsworth, and he gave me £16.75 change. It wasn't even a Catholic church in the end, but a Born Again church.

> Anyway, luckily there was a Filipina there, and she had worked for a Middle Eastern family too, and she had run away. She told me she knew about an organisation that helped people like us, and she put me in touch with the centre.

British immigration laws criminalise women who escape from their employers, in that they soon become 'unauthorised workers', 'overstayers' or both, and liable to deportation. In fact, they may be overstayers (ie have spent longer in Britain that their visa permits without any extension) even before leaving their employers, since it is usually the employer who negotiates their conditions of entry, and the employer who holds their passport, so the women are ignorant of their conditions of entry. In any event, the women are 'working in breach' (of their conditions of entry) as soon as they find work with another employer, because, even if they have been given permission to work under Code 4, they are not allowed to change employer. Most, as we have seen, have no permission to work at all. Despite the risk, they must work, children and families still need to be fed. As illustrated above many workers who escape abusive employers have incurred large debts to find work abroad and have been paid irregularly, less than promised or not at all. All this adds up to greater financial problems than they had before they left home and therefore a greater urgency to find work.

As in Kuwait, having run away from her employer Alice could not work legally for anyone else, just as, as in Kuwait her working conditions were unprotected by employment laws since she qualified as a household member rather than an employee. The dependence enforced by immigration and employment laws remained the same in Britain as in Kuwait, enabling her employers to exercise the same power over her. The difference, she explains, was that it was easier for her to run away in Britain because her employer was not in his own country:

> It is very easy for them to trace you in the Middle East, especially if they are high ranking like my employer, so you cannot run away.

For those women who have escaped, the new situation brings with it then its own difficulties. There is of course the inevitable trauma to be faced having endured such conditions of abuse, and the fear of recapture. There are practical problems, where to find accommodation, clothes, borrow a little money. All these difficulties are compounded by their immigration status.

A domestic who runs away can receive no support from the state: if sick, she can claim no benefit or health care; if attacked she cannot go to the police; she has

---

Kalpana's Story

Kalpana worked in a factory in Bombay as did her husband. Together they were barely able to support themselves and their three children. Catastrophe occurred when her husband had an accident and was no longer able to work. Not only were they suddenly without his income but they immediately incurred medical expenses which outweighed Kalpana's income.

A friend put Kalpana in touch with an agency which said that, for a fee, they could get her a job abroad which would give her more than enough income to pay for the medical expenses and take care of her family. Kalpana's husband was reluctant to allow her to go abroad but other members of her family supported her saying it was the only way. The family was only able to borrow the fee by mortgaging the small plot of land they owned at very high interest rates.

Kalpana was given a job as a domestic worker in Qatar. The life she experienced there was far from what was promised by the agency. The salary she was promised by the agency was never paid to her. She was made to work around the clock with little food and no time off, was constantly shouted at, insulted and occasionally beaten.

More than a year later she was finally able to escape from her employers during a visit to London. All she could think of was finding work to pay off the debt which was still unpaid and accumulating interest and to send some money home to feed her family.

Eighteen months after leaving her employer her debt was paid and Kalpana was able to return to her family.

no means of redress or complaint at unfair employment practices. An unauthorised worker cannot go home for a visit because she will not be allowed back into Britain – and this in particular is a source of great distress when a close relative dies. Lulu's young daughter died, but she could not go back to be with her other children and her husband, because she had to continue earning money for their survival. The day of her daughter's funeral she scrubbed and polished as usual, she went to the park with her employer's little girl, and cried as she watched over her in the playground. Her family, like many, do not know that she is unauthorised and could not understand why she did not return home. Such a situation is not unusual.

Even opening a bank account is problematic because of the requirement for proof of identity – but if their hard earned money is stolen from them, they cannot go to the police. The women continue to work extremely long hours, this time pressurised not only or even necessarily by exacting employers, but because of their legal situation. As Alice said:

> *I must work all the time because tomorrow maybe I will be picked up and sent home, or maybe I will be ill, and cannot earn any money for weeks, because we are not eligible for any kind of benefit.*

Life is particularly difficult if a worker becomes sick. If she cannot work, she cannot earn money. However legitimate the reason, employers can always sack her if she does not turn up for work, and she has no redress. Doctors and hospitals often ask for passports, thereby deterring all but the most seriously ill, who on their recovery can be faced with a large bill and a deportation order.

The fear of discovery is a constant source of stress – an unexpected knock on the door could always be the prelude to instant deportation:

> *Because of my situation fear is with me constantly and I even give false names to my employers. They do not know about my real situation. I'm longing to have a holiday back home, but I can't do it because of my illegal position. Sometimes in the middle of the night I just lie awake thinking that one day the immigration officer will come and get me. Worse of all, I can't even trust a friend, thinking that they might tip off the immigration authorities about me.*

It is difficult for unauthorised workers to form friendships because of their situation. The women are extremely isolated because they are vulnerable to anybody who knows their secret, who can extort money and services from them whether they be acquaintances, landlords, or of course, employers:

> *I work for an English family and I start at 6am. I'm supposed to have a break at 2pm, but if you live in you can't get away from the responsibility, and besides, I am taking care of the baby, which they say is a rest, but that's not a rest, you still have the responsibility. They call on me whenever they want. I finish at 10pm. It is hard as a TNT* [11]*, you must work so hard, you're tired all the time,*

so you don't feel like eating and you get ill. I want to learn English so I can defend myself with my employers. I want to stay here legally, but as it is we are not like human beings. You cannot share your own problems. I can't tell you what will happen in the next few days. Sometimes I had a very wicked thought, I want to kill myself, I think my mind will burst with my problems. I told my friend and she said, 'But it is very nice to live'.

The dilemma the women find themselves in is clearly illustrated by Helen, who is facing deportation having run away from her employers in Bexleyheath on the outskirts of London. She was brought to Britain from the south of Nigeria six years ago, when she was nineteen, and endured years of abuse. She was forced to sleep outside the back door, even in winter, and was dressed only in rags. Her food consisted mainly of unripe apples and pears from the garden and the three children's leftovers – she had been 'hired' originally as a child-minder. She even resorted to writing begging notes for food and throwing them over the fence. Helen was kicked and beaten by her employer, who was a doctor, and on one occasion he 'stabbed' her back repeatedly with a safety pin until her T-shirt was speckled all over with blood. His wife told her to stop bleeding on the carpet. She admitted gouging Helen's face with her nails and pulling her hair out. Helen still bears the marks on her throat where she tried to strangle her. Her day began at 6 am and did not end until her abusers decided it could. Her torment came to an end in September 1989 when she ran bleeding to a next door neighbour. She weighed about six and a half stone and was suffering from malnutrition; there were whip marks and cuts and scratches all over her body. In November 1991, Helen was awarded damages for assault, but was faced with deportation as an overstayer. Helen's case, though ultimately successful, illustrates how risky and difficult it is for domestic workers to seek recourse to British justice. The withholding of wages and the other factors already discussed make it impossible for women who have escaped to return home. Either already illegal or facing imminent illegality under the immigration laws, the vast majority of abused women decide not to risk the exposure to the state that litigation will inevitably bring.

For all the difficulties inherent in their situation, the runaway domestics are not simply passive victims of circumstance. They have worked together and provided mutual emotional support. They have also won the support of large sections of British public opinion, and together with campaigning and voluntary organisations have even secured some minor improvements from the Home Office.

1 Hansard Vol 178, WA col. 735, 1st November 1990; Hansard Vol 183 col. 189-90 WA 19th December 1990.
2 Letter from The Foreign and Commonwealth Office in reply to an enquiry from Cardinal Hume, 29th September 1992.

3 Bhabha J., Klug K., and Shutter S., 1985. *World's Apart: Women Under Immigration and Nationality Law*, London: Pluto Press.
4 Parliamentary Select Committee 1977.
5 Quoted in the booklet accompanying Kalayaan's Open Space film *Domestic Slavery*, broadcast on BBC2, 16th November 1987.
6 'Instructions' are secret and are issued to immigration officials containing criteria and reasons for making decisions. They are regularly updated by the Home Office with no reference to any outside body. They are not published.
7 Sue Shutter of The Joint Council for the Welfare of Immigrants speaking on Kalayaan's Open Space film.
8 Hansard col. 1052, 28th November 1990, House of Lords Debate on Overseas Domestic Workers.
9 Ibid col. 1045.
10 Ibid col. 1039.
11 TNT stands for 'Tago ng tago', Tagalog for 'Hide and hide'; It is a term used by Filipino unauthorised workers all over the world to describe themselves.

CHAPTER FOUR

Kalayaan Means Freedom!
Campaigning in Britain

When I arrived in London I was locked inside the house. I had no key of my own and I could not go out. They told me not to go out of the house and not to let anybody inside. I was afraid to do anything. I wanted to leave them but I was afraid of what the family could do to me. I was also afraid to run away because I did not know anybody here in London. I did not know of anybody who could help me.[1]

Alone, it is very difficult for a woman to resolve the practical and emotional problems of escaping from an abusive situation. She is vulnerable to deportation and exploitation, does not know whom she can trust, and certainly cannot ask for any legislative changes to ease her situation.

Commission For Filipino Migrant Workers

The Commission for Filipino Migrant Workers (CFMW) is an organisation established in 1979 to serve the needs of the Filipino migrant community in Britain, which particularly emphasises its role as a facilitator and supporter of groups organised by Filipinos themselves. It participated in the successful campaign against the deportation of some 400 Filipino women in 1980-81, and played a leading role in a successful coalition against enforced remittances, which the Philippine government had attempted to implement in 1983. It also facilitated the establishment of several local Filipino groups.

From 1984 onwards, CFMW noticed a trend emerging from those Filipinos who were seeking their support and advice: a number of individuals were coming to them with similar problems, with no passport, unpaid wages, no belongings and disturbing reports of brutal conditions. In 1985 they invited a small number of women to meet to discuss these problems and see what could be done about them. When the women shared their experiences it became apparent that this was a much bigger issue than had previously been thought. CFMW suggested they discuss setting up a support network for those arriving without any contacts in London. This was agreed, and it was also decided to meet regularly to learn about their legal rights as well as discuss their individual problems.

Mahesh Kumari Rai left her home in a Nepalese mountain village at the age of thirteen to avoid an arranged marriage. After work as a carpet weaver in Kathmandu she made her way to Delhi, India, where she found domestic work. It was then, in 1984, that a family enticed her to accompany them to London where she would have a good job as their housekeeper. The situation that Mahesh experienced in London was not the easy life with good pay and a chance for an education which she had been promised; instead it was long hours, imprisonment, no pay at all, no education and constant physical and psychological abuse. It was a life of virtual slavery.

Two years after arriving in Britain, Mahesh managed to escape and with the help of a law centre she took her former employer to court for compensation and her unpaid wages. The matter was settled out of court. Mahesh received £1,349 – the equivalent of £13 a week.

For the two years Mahesh was with them, her former employers had neglected to keep her visa in order; she was therefore liable for deportation. Mahesh did not fully understand her immigration situation. She remained in Britain for several years, establishing a full life here with many friends; she had a job with a good family; and she attended English classes.

In April 1991, Mahesh was picked up and taken to Harmondsworth Detention Centre. Kalayaan who knew of Mahesh became actively involved. A campaign was mounted to release Mahesh and to encourage the Home Office to take the exceptional circumstances of Mahesh's situation into account and allow her stay.

Kalayaan working with Mahesh's lawyer and with the backing of more than 25 MP's, several peers and other public figures and organisations, including Anti-Slavery International, managed to secure her release but not until she had been in jail for six months. The campaign continued. Many MP's wrote several times on her behalf urging the Home Office to look closely at Mahesh's circumstances and reconsider. Kalayaan co-ordinated a widespread media campaign generating newspaper articles and radio interviews. Hundreds of individuals signed Kalayaan's petition to encourage the Home Office to allow Mahesh to stay. Her lawyer obtained a judicial review which ordered the Home Office to prove that it had taken account of Mahesh's circumstances and the representations on her behalf. In reply the Home Office simply stated this had been done and gave no further explanation.

In August 1992 Mahesh received notice that the Home Office was refusing her the right to remain in the UK and would be acting on the deportation order. Mahesh was jailed for two more months while awaiting deportation and despite all efforts to stop this, including an intervention by Cardinal Hume, Mahesh was deported to Nepal where she had neither family nor friends and had not been for more than fifteen years.

At the time of writing, four months after her deportation, Mahesh is still without work and has no money.

Trust and friendships soon developed; in the words of one woman:

> *I went back to normal. Before, when I was alone, I didn't trust anyone. My experience with my employers meant that I couldn't speak up. It makes you silent and not open. When I began to talk to people in similar situations, and I saw that I was not alone, I realised that the problem was not just to do with me, that it was the Philippines and Britain and the government in those countries.*

Amongst unauthorised domestic workers in Britain, the majority are Filipinos, but there are also Nepalese, Indian, Sri Lankan, Nigerian, Mauritian and others. The invasion of Kuwait, and the subsequent Gulf War, increased the number of workers leaving their employers. From August to November 1990 there was an average of 80 to 90 workers a month who felt forced to flee. Many of their employers had used 'frozen assets' as a reason for not paying them.

Women who have just escaped their employers can find practical and emotional help through CFMW. They are found a place to stay and have access to a small amount of money to help with immediate needs. They meet other people who can help them through their emotional trauma because they have shared experiences. This sympathy and understanding is crucial in rebuilding the self-respect of women who have been systematically degraded and treated as less than human. It is a process which in turn enables those women to help others. All this gives the women a breathing space, time to recover from their trauma, and importantly, the possibility of making a decision on their next step, informed by sound legal advice.

But all this is not enough. It can only make the workers' situation more tolerable. There is still the ever present fear of deportation, of sickness which will prevent them from earning, of illness or death in the family back home. And of course, there are still the unknown numbers who cannot escape. The only way of solving these kinds of problems is to change the law. All these considerations made it clear that a separate campaign and support group was necessary (see box opposite).

Kalayaan

Kalayaan, 'Freedom' in the Philippine language Tagalog, was established on 16th June 1987 to work for the rights of all overseas domestic workers, and specifically for the right to an immigration status independent of their employers, one that recognised their status as workers, their right to change employers and their right to normal work benefits and health care. It is the public face of unauthorised domestic workers, raising the profile of the issue and helping to support other groups and service agencies around it. Kalayaan also concerns itself with the practical needs of the workers. As well as helping workers to get settled and find a safe place to stay, it runs English classes, helps train legal advisers, provides workers with legal support for the repossession of their passports, their unpaid wages etc. It draws its members from migrant and immigrant support groups, trade unions, law centres and migrant organisations, as well as concerned individuals.

The Political Lobby

Kalayaan was fortunate in quickly winning the support of the late Sir Brandon Rhys Williams MP, whose Kensington North constituency contained many employers and their servants. With his help, members of the campaign were able to meet Mr Timothy Renton, Minister of State for the Home Office, and representatives of the Department of Employment and the Foreign Office.

The Minister's original response, in a letter dated 27th October 1988 seemed promising:

> *I do sympathise with domestic servants admitted under the arrangements ....who nevertheless find their conditions of employment intolerable....we remain concerned about this problem and I am open to suggestions as to changes we could make in our immigration control to improve the situation.*[2]

In 1989 he was still expressing his concern, when he wrote to Dudley Fishburn MP, who had succeeded Sir Brandon Rhys Williams in his constituency:

> *I share your concern about Filipino domestic servants... who find their conditions of work intolerable.*[3]

Both Kalayaan and CFMW were encouraged: the Home Office at least recognised that there was a problem, and was open to suggestions on suitable changes to immigration practice, even if they had no solutions themselves. On 15th October 1989 the issue was brought to the wider attention of the House of Commons, when an Early Day Motion was introduced by Conservative MP, David Evenett. This is a means traditionally used by MP's to draw their colleagues' and the government's attention to matters of importance. Early Day Motion 1216 was signed by 104 MP's from all parties, including Harry Greenway, Conservative MP for Ealing North and Tony Benn, Labour MP for Chesterfield. It read:

> *That this House notes with concern the plight of some overseas domestic workers brought into the United Kingdom by their employers; and calls upon the Secretary of State for the Home Department to ensure that all domestic workers from overseas are provided with a suitable immigration status which enables them to work legally and change employers whilst in the United Kingdom, and which will help to end the maltreatment and abuse of overseas domestic workers by some employers.*

A further 14 MP's signed an addition:

> *and therefore urges the Government to include the necessary regulation or legislation needed to bring about such a change in immigration status in the*

forthcoming Queen's Speech.

A few weeks later in December 1989, the High Court awarded Mrs Laxmi Swami £300,000 damages against her employer. It seemed as if justice was going to be done.

On 20th March 1990, Kalayaan and the Commission for Filipino Migrant Workers met officials from the Home Office and Lord Strathclyde from the Department of Employment. This was arranged and attended by Lord Hylton, a consistent supporter of the campaign for overseas domestic workers. The principal point that was put to the Home Office at this meeting was that workers should be given the right to change employers within their existing employment category (ie as long as they continued to work as domestics). Other suggestions included a requirement that a written contract of employment, enforceable in the UK, be signed by employers and employees staying more than a certain period in UK; and that there should be an amnesty for those women who had escaped from their employer and found other work, providing they had already spent four years in the UK.

This position was clarified in a forum sponsored by the Commission for Racial Equality on 11th July 1990. This was coordinated by Kalayaan and attended by CFMW, Anti-Slavery International and the Joint Council for the Welfare of Immigrants, as well as interested individuals. Domestic workers from India and the Philippines who three years before would have been in hiding and unable to reveal their immigration status to anyone took the platform and spoke of their ordeals before a large audience: Sally told of her escape from a Kensington house after years of abuse and degradation by her employers. She was kept imprisoned, and had to climb down a drainpipe to escape. She was discovered by the porter some two hours later, lying in a pool of blood, having fallen from the second floor and broken her arm and her pelvis. Her life when she came out of hospital was still hard; she worked for six days a week from 8am to 6pm for two different employers every day, and from 7pm to 1.30am she worked as a garment piece-worker in her room. 'I want to save money and if I can save money then I can go home.'

Confronted by experiences like this, the forum agreed the following resolutions as the basis for discussions with the Home Office:

1. This forum seeks either a change in the Immigration Rules or a concession to mirror that already offered to employers; the beneficiaries would be people who came to the United Kingdom in circumstances where it was clear on arrival that they were already recruited as domestics and were coming to the United Kingdom to work in that capacity.
2. Such persons should be able to change employers if their employment continues to be within a similar field of occupation.
3. After four years of any such employment such persons should be able to claim

settlement in the United Kingdom.

4. Those persons who entered the United Kingdom as in (1) and then left their employers and have now overstayed their leave to remain in the United Kingdom should have their position regularised, bringing them within the terms of the concession.

Pressure was maintained on the Home Office in the House of Commons where six Parliamentary Questions were raised on the issue in 1990. The campaign could claim the support of some 250 MP's. There was also mounting international pressure which was being encouraged through the work of Anti-Slavery International.

Anti-Slavery International

The Anti-Slavery Society was formed in 1839 from the previous groups opposed to enslavement, and is the world's oldest international human rights organisation. Now called Anti-Slavery International (ASI),[4] it is the only organisation seeking to eliminate all forms of traditional and modern slavery, and has no doubts that foreign domestic workers in the same positions as Alice, Laxmi, and Sally, come under their remit:

> *A slave is anybody who is denied the possibility of controlling his or her own life... You ought to be able to take certain decisions, and I think many of these domestic servants simply do not have that possibility. They're habitually on call twenty four hours a day, seven days a week, no holidays, completely at the beck and call of the master or mistress. Yes, I think they can certainly be called slaves.*[5]

ASI's first experience of the problem had been in 1977, when they gave evidence to the United Nations on two cases of slavery in diplomats' households. As a consequence of the publicity surrounding these cases, more were brought to them, and in 1984 the subject was again raised by the Society before the UN Economic and Social Council's Working Group on Slavery:

> *Twice in recent years I have been given evidence of slave-owning by persons of diplomatic status living or staying in the West End of London. In one case the matron of a well-known clinic was required to allow a patient to have his slave sleeping on the floor in his doorway. Believing that the slave was about to break down for lack of rest, the matron offered to provide a relief. 'She stays here at my pleasure. There are plenty more where she comes from' was the reply.*
>
> *In an adjacent street a girl emerged briefly from a diplomat's flat to seize an opportunity to show to the wife of a friend of mine bite marks on her arm and a brand mark on the crown of her head. My friend's flat was in the same house.*

They saw her on several occasions being dragged out screaming to be lent to the diplomat's men-friends.

The police declined to take action. Discreet diplomatic action caused the diplomat to move. The case remained unknown to the public. The basic ill remained.[6]

Diplomats of course are protected not only by wealth and privilege, but also by diplomatic immunity. ASI's 1984 submission, in the words of one of its members:

slowly made its way through five layers of bureaucracy until it came to rest on a shelf in the Palais des Nations, never to be read again.

The iron curtain of diplomatic immunity proved to be impenetrable and it was felt that more immediate success would arise from looking at the wider problem of domestic slavery in non-diplomatic households. In 1990, ASI detailed the problems of migrant domestic workers in the UK before the UN, and stated strongly that:

the effects of the Immigration Acts as they touch upon overseas domestic workers, the non-issuance of work permits to these workers, and the effective treatment of these workers by the immigration authorities as appendages of the employer rather than as individuals in their own right, to be responsible for the servitude these domestics suffer in Britain. The Home Office, however inadvertently, is supporting slavery.[7]

In his meeting of March 1990 with the Home Office, Lord Hylton referred to the potential embarrassment caused to the British Government by these kinds of revelations.

Speaking Out

While recognising the importance of national and international lobby work however, one should not underestimate the even more crucial support of the general public for the campaign. The plight of domestic workers was first brought to general attention in June 1987, by a Face the Facts programme with Kalayaan on BBC Radio 4. Some months later, in November, the workers and their support groups made an Open Space Film for BBC 2. The making of the programme was in itself an achievement, as women found the courage to 'go public', and one worker even risked deportation and allowed her face to be shown:

I decided to appear in this programme because I wanted to tell my story, and I want the British people and the British government to know what is happening to us and how they can help. Not only Filipinos like us but other people, other nationalities who are in the same kind of situation. How can we be helped? What can they do for us? That is why I decided to appear in front of the camera on this programme.[8]

In response to the film, Kalayaan and the BBC received over nine hundred telephone calls. The campaign has continued to receive extensive press coverage, not just TV, but radio, newspapers and magazines, both locally and nationally, have taken up the issue.[9] This has entailed a lot of work for Kalayaan, CFMW, and the escaped workers. It is, moreover, a constant battle on the one hand to preserve the privacy and anonymity of the women and put across the point of view of the campaign, and on the other to tell personal stories which can convey the issue. A clear example of this is the media coverage of the case of Mahesh Kumari Rai (see page 58). Although one of the most difficult areas of work it has proved very rewarding, and Kalayaan obtained over 4,000 signatories for her in its petition to the Home Secretary.

Home Office Response

On 24th July 1990 the Home Office announced its regret that causes of abuse and exploitation should have occurred, and the imposition of new controls to minimise abuse.

These were:

1. All domestic servants will be required to obtain entry clearance before coming here. The entry clearance officer will carefully consider the individual circumstances of each application and will refuse entry clearance unless he is satisfied about the bona fides of the domestic arrangement and that it comes within the terms of the concession.
2. The domestic servant must have been in continuous, paid employment with the employer abroad for at least the previous 12 months before coming with a visitor or at least two years in all other cases.
3. The minimum age at which a domestic servant will be granted entry clearance is 17 years.
4. Information leaflets will be issued both to employers and domestics at the entry clearance stage, setting out the legal rights of domestics working here and the protection available to them under United Kingdom law.[10]

Unfortunately, none of these measures tackled the root cause of the problem, which is not the 'bona fides' of the relationship. Nor is the insistence of previous employment by the same employer any help – as has been seen, many of the domestics who come to Britain have been suffering extreme cruelty from their employer for a number of years. Although there have been cases of children being brought to Britain as domestic workers, point 3 is not adequate to prevent even this and it is certainly no help in tackling the general problems faced by domestic workers.

Kalayaan, ASI and other supportive parties were consulted on the information leaflet mentioned in point 4, but its final draft and distribution were heavily

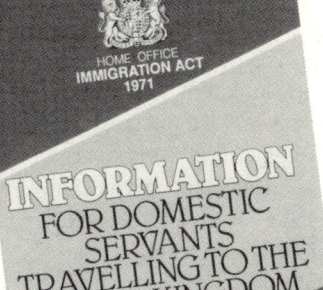

HOME OFFICE
IMMIGRATION ACT
1971

[NO]TICE TO EMPLOYERS OF
[DOMES]TIC SERVANTS TRAVELLING
[TO] THE UNITED KINGDOM

[The a]ttached information leaflet has been [given to mem]bers of your domestic staff who have [to accom]pany you on your forthcoming visit to [the United Kingdo]m. The leaflet explains the [condit]ions attached to the stay of domestic workers there, and their rights under criminal and employment law. The vast majority of overseas employers look after their domestic workers well. However from time to time allegations are made that employers treat domestic workers in ways which conflict with United Kingdom law.

The leaflet explains that domestic workers have certain rights in the United Kingdom even though their stay is subject to conditions. It also acknowledges that domestics may find themselves isolated in the United Kingdom, unable to speak the language. Its purpose is to explain in simple terms where they can find help, should they require it for any reason.

Home Office leaflets issued to employers and domestics

criticised by Kalayaan in their annual summary report 1991, which concluded:

> *The leaflet is an entirely cosmetic exercise and ignores the documented reality of the widespread systematic abuse of the workers.*[11]

The leaflet's purpose was allegedly to prevent abuses of domestics workers by employers, yet it was aimed, not at the abusers, but at the workers. Indeed, because it laid its principal emphasis on the employee's immigration situation, and made it clear that in law, a domestic servant can work for nobody other than their abusing employer, it was felt by the campaign to only encourage exploitation. Moreover, out of 20 domestic workers who had fled their employers and subsequently been interviewed by CFMW in July 1992, 14 had not been given any leaflet. Of the six leaflets that were given out, one was taken from the domestic worker by the employer as soon as the entry clearance interview was over. Furthermore according to CFMW's research about one third of entry clearance interviews take place with the employer present while others are threatened and told by the employers what answers to give.

The Home Office position had obviously hardened. In a debate on Overseas Domestic Workers in the House of Lords on 28th November 1990, Lord Reay, speaking for the government affirmed:

> *The Government do not accept the suggestion that it is the concession itself which in some way creates the problems that have arisen.......the conditions for work permit holders are in line with those for overseas domestic workers who come here under the concession, and there would be no practical advantage at all in bringing domestic workers within the work permit arrangements.*

> *Another suggestion which is made is that we should at least allow domestic workers to change employers here. The government cannot accept that. Domestic workers are admitted in this exceptional way in order to safeguard their livelihoods.*[12]

This is a far cry from Timothy Renton's 1988 statements.

The government's line was reiterated in a letter to Lord Hylton from the Home Office on 5th February 1991 which admitted concern 'about the cases where domestic workers have apparently been abused.' A note of doubt as to whether the cases of abuse and exploitation even take place has been introduced into the argument.

Further attempts to encourage the Home Office to at least recognise that the problem continues to exist have been met with evasion. On 7th December 1992 Lord Monkswell put a question to the Government in the House of Lords asking that it:

Results of Survey

The table below represents the results of a survey carried out by the Commission for Filipino Migrant Workers. Two hundred and forty seven people were canvassed from 17 different nationalities, representing all those overseas domestic workers who left their employers and sought help from CFMW from February 1992 to September 1992. The table lists the percentage of those workers interviewed who had experienced nine different forms of abuse commonly encountered.

Psychological Abuse (threats, name calling, constant shouting, insults)	89.1%
Physical Abuse (hitting, shoving, spitting, kicking, beating etc. by any member of the household)	31.4%
Sexual Abuse (attempted, threatened, or actual rape)	8.6%
Regular Denial of Food (given food only if there is any left over from an employer's plate, regularly made to go without food – not including forced fasting)	61.3%
Not Having a Bedroom (made to sleep in the hall, kitchen, toilet, etc.)	51.4%
Not Having a Bed	52.3%
Imprisonment (being denied permission to leave the house at all or without accompaniment)	26.3%
Confiscation of Passport (and not obtainable on departure from employer's home)	83.2%
Not Paid Regularly, As Promised, or At All	74%

In addition, the survey found that respondents worked on average 18-19 hours every day and that days off almost never existed; indeed, workers were rarely allowed time for meals. The average fee paid to recruitment agencies was US$216 (primarily in the Philippines where the average annual per capita income is US$600).

> *list, by Police Authority, for each of the last five years, how many complaints to the police were made by overseas domestic workers in the UK about their employer or members of their employer's family; how many prosecutions resulted; and how many convictions resulted.*

In reply for the Government, Earl Ferrers answered that the information was not available.[13]

The Home Office continues the line of doubt and further removes itself from responsibility claiming that it is a police matter; in a letter dated 25th January 1993, the official line is reiterated:

> *(overseas domestics are) entitled to the full protection of the criminal laws and can complain to the police if they are physically abused or are in any way deprived of their liberty.*[14]

The Home Office uses the leaflet as the overriding defence to claim it has done all it can; this is most recently spelt out in the same letter of January 1993 :

> *We trust these new arrangements will minimise the scope for abuse of domestics by their employers...*[15]

But as we have seen, the Home Office make no provisions for domestic workers to be granted leave to remain while they pursue legal action, civil or criminal. Government representatives are then obliged to argue in immigration tribunals that, while on the one hand they have no doubt that atrocities did in fact happen, the workers may not be granted leave to remain to see their case through the courts. This has occurred in the case of an Indian worker who is taking action against her former employers but is at the same time having to fight to stay here to do this.

Legal avenues for redress are notoriously difficult to pursue. The right to redress for a domestic worker seeking compensation for non-payment of wages and for the various kinds of abuse we have chronicled lies through the civil Courts.

When overseas domestic workers seek legal advice they discover the precariousness of their position in the UK. Advisers will inevitably tell them that no matter how compelling and strong their case is in law, there is no guarantee that they will be allowed to stay in the UK to pursue the claim. We know of very few who have been granted exceptional leave in this situation to remain, and many have been refused such leave.

There is the further twist arising from the fact that, without their wages, overseas domestic workers are unable to repay the original debt usually incurred when setting out from home to seek work.

The campaign to redress the situation faced by overseas domestic workers has not been limited to Britain. In a 1991 conference of the Filipino migrant community in Europe, special attention was drawn to the economic and social contribution of the tens of thousands of undocumented domestic helpers in Europe:

> *Every single domestic helper and/or baby sitter liberates at least one European, mainly women, to become active in the labour force.*
>
> *The contribution of the non-EC migrants, immigrants and refugees, especially to the economy of Europe should be given its due recognition.*
>
> *We are against the criminalization of the undocumented migrant workers through the creation of the TREVI 1992 Group and their inclusion in the Schengen Information System. This is unjust and uncalled for.*
>
> *The economic and social rights and welfare of the non-EC migrants, immigrants and refugees should be included in the social package of Europe 1992. We also deserve to benefit from the fruits of our labour.*

The conference called for the recognition of their rights to freedom of movement and work, to family reunification and permanent residence and to vote. The following demands for unauthorised workers were also put:

> *that undocumented migrant workers be given proper working papers and due benefits and the protection of the social welfare system;*
>
> *that any undocumented migrant arrested be treated with respect for her/his human rights;*
>
> *that internal controls – such as police spot checking of individuals in public places and/or in the houses, in hospitals etc. – on the basis of race or color of the skin be prohibited.*

The Conference concluded:

> *Together with other migrants, immigrants and refugees, we want a JUST, DEMOCRATIC, MULTICULTURAL EUROPE.*

For, while the concession is specific to the United Kingdom, the position of migrant domestic workers elsewhere in Europe is similarly marked by exploitation and abuse.

---

1 Former domestic worker speaking on *Domestic Slavery*, Kalayaan's Open Space film, broadcast on BBC2, 16th November 1987.
2 Letter to Mr Michael Day OBE, Commission for Racial Equality, 27th October 1988.
3 Letter dated 22nd May 1989.
4 The name was changed in November 1990.
5 Peter Davies, Director of the then Anti-Slavery Society speaking on Kalayaan's Open Space film, 1987.
6 Statement by Patrick Montgomery, member of the then Anti-Slavery Society's General Committee, before the United Nations Working Group on Contemporary Forms of Slavery, 31st July 1984. (UN Economic and Social Council, Commission on Human Rights, Sub-Commission on

Prevention of Discrimination and Protection of Minorities, Working Group on Contemporary Forms of Slavery, Tenth Session, Geneva, 1984)

7 *Domestic Workers*, 1990. Anti-Slavery Society Report to the United Nations Working Group on Contemporary Forms of Slavery. (UN Economic and Social Council, Commission on Human Rights, Sub-Commission on Prevention of Discrimination and Protection of Minorities, Working Group on Contemporary Forms of Slavery, Fifteenth Session, Geneva, 1990 – text in Appendix II).

8 Kalayaan's Open Space film, 1987.

9 Media coverage includes:
- BBC Radio 4: Face the Facts, 4th June 1987;
- BBC 2: Open Space, 16th November 1987;
- The Guardian and Asian Times: feature articles, 1988;
- BBC News London South East, December 1989;
- The Independent, 12th December 1989;
- Channel 4: Orientations, 1st January 1990;
- The Observer Magazine, 28th January 1990;
- The Guardian, 16th April 1990;
- The Independent, 16th April 1990;
- Granada TV: World in Action, June 1991;
- The Independent, November 1991-February 1992: a series of articles called 'Slavery in Britain';
- BBC Radio 4: PM, 27th August 1992.

10 The full text of the Home Office leaflet is transcribed in Appendix III.

11 Kalayaan's Summary Report, AGM 21st September 1991.

12 Hansard col.1052, 28th November 1990, House of Lords debate on Overseas Domestic Workers.

13 Hansard Vol. 541, WA4.

14 Letter from the Immigration and Nationality Department, Home Office, to ASI, 25th January 1993 (text in Appendix IV).

15 Ibid.

CHAPTER FIVE

The Hidden State: The European Dimension

There is a hidden, thirteenth state in the European Community (EC): the 16 million migrants, immigrants and refugees who live and work in Europe[1]. Together they number more than the combined population of Belgium and Denmark, but they are denied the 'freedom' of the new Europe. For third world workers, both in Britain and in the EC as a whole, the much vaunted 'Europe 1992' promises more difficulties not greater freedom; many of them are domestic workers.

The drive towards a single European market, which has increased the mobility within the EC of its Member States' citizens, has meant instead, increasing restrictions for migrant workers over the past few years. They cannot vote in local and national elections, in some countries they cannot form political organisations, and they are often not allowed to take jobs in the public sector. And yet the economies of the EC members are increasingly dependent on this cheap, flexible labour force. It provides the agricultural seasonal workers, the factory and mine workers, the fast food cooks, the garment workers, and of course the domestic workers. These are the low status, low paid jobs, vulnerable to exploitation. They are an unprotected population, whose rights are often not addressed by the national legislation of either the receiving states or their states of origin, and who are not given a mention in the 12 basic principles of the EC's Social Charter.[2]

Migration and Europe

Something like 30 million people entered the Western European countries as workers or workers' dependents in the post-war period, making this one of the greatest migratory movements in human history. Many did indeed return to their countries of origin after a while, but others stayed. Immigration of workers was not of course the only migratory current of Western Europe in this period. In the late forties and early fifties there was considerable overseas migration, leading to a net loss for the whole of Europe of three million people. Europe gained population as colonists returned from countries like India, Algeria, Angola and Mozambique. The aftermath of the Second World War and beginning of the cold war caused large-scale refugee movements. But labour migration was the largest factor in the development of immigrant populations.[3]

Following the Second World War, European countries, particularly those in the North, began to look abroad for a solution to their shortage of labour. The countries they turned to depended largely on their history and their current economic links. Thus Britain and Holland looked to their colonies and ex-colonies; France to Algeria, and later to Morocco and Tunisia; and West Germany first to Poland and the GDR, and then to the Mediterranean, to Turkey, Italy, Yugoslavia and Greece. In general this massive movement of people was organised by the European states and employers. It was usually controlled by the 'guestworker' system instituted after the war, whereby a special government department was set up to recruit workers for employers. As in the Gulf states and in the UK under the work permit system, migrants were tied to a specific job and employer for a specific time, and had to leave the country if they were sacked. They also had to leave the country at the end of their contract. These people provided a convenient, disposable labour force: the European nations had contributed nothing to their upkeep while they were young and unproductive, but they came 'ready made'.

In Southern Europe the story was slightly different: Italy, Spain and Portugal were originally labour exporting countries, both within Europe and to the United States and Canada. Today there are more than five million Italians dispersed throughout the world; during the 1960s more than one million Spaniards sought work in the booming industrial economies of Northern Europe. In fact, until the mid-70s, Spanish women came to Britain to work in the same sectors as Filipinas – in the hotel and catering industry and as domestics in private homes and hospitals. In 1961 75 per cent of Spanish women in Britain were working as domestics.

Like other migrants, those from Southern Europe during this time had to endure the racism of their host countries:

> 'A large number of bars in Brussels,' wrote a young Spanish lawyer called Felipe Gonzalez, who was studying temporarily in Belgium at the time, 'had an announcement: no entry for Spaniards, Africans and North Africans....the railway stations are packed with Spaniards who spend hour upon hour in a state of disorientation. They're not shown the slightest consideration and are in the saddest human and spiritual misery.'[4]

The post-1973 recession following the oil crisis in Europe drove Southern Europeans back to their countries of origin; more recently, increased prosperity has changed the countries of Southern Europe into host countries for immigration. The experiences of their own migrants in Northern Europe has not ensured better treatment for those who come from the Third World to work in Southern Europe – 'How many doors have I had slammed in my face because I was black.'[5] Because of their proximity to Africa, and their recent, relatively lax immigration policies, together with a reputation for 'leaky frontiers', the Southern European members of the EC have come to be regarded as an alarming bridgehead into Europe; in recent years, they have responded to a great deal of pressure to tighten their immigration controls. All of this has had a direct impact on the lives of domestic workers.

Spain

According to estimates in 1991, there are some 800,000 non-European migrants in Spain working in textile factories, mines, construction sites and the informal economy. The majority of them are from Latin America, followed by North Africa and the Philippines. Over 300,000 do not have immigration documents.

It is estimated that just over one third of migrants are women and for them the single largest area of employment is domestic work. In fact domestic work is an important area of employment for Spanish women as well, accounting for more female employment than any other area of the Spanish labour market – 16.5 per cent of female workers in 1985, or approximately half a million women. Among Spanish nationals who are domestic servants 60 per cent are working in the 'black economy'. Because it is in the very nature of domestic work to be invisible, domestic service attracts large numbers of unauthorised workers. It is scarcely surprising then, that for foreign domestics, anxious to preserve their security, the rate of illegality is even higher. In 1986 there were an estimated 32,000 overseas domestics in Spain. Only 7,000 of those, or under 20 per cent were legal.

In Spain as throughout the world, domestic work is not given its proper place, but is systematically discriminated against. Domestic workers are considered in Spanish employment law as a special category, working and yet not working, and therefore not deserving of the same rights as other workers. This institutionalised discrimination is well illustrated by the different social security arrangements for domestic employees.

There is legislation outlining maximum hours (40 per week) and minimum pay of 388 pesetas (£2) per hour for domestics, but such laws are notoriously difficult to enforce, particularly for live-in workers. This is precisely the area of work that Spanish women are leaving, preferring to work on a daily basis, or paid by the hour, and they are being replaced by women from the developing world and Portugal.

On the employers' side, there are advantages in having an illegal worker whom one can pay below the minimum wage, not pay contributions for, and control more closely:

> *They treat you like a slave..... it goes on like this, they threaten you, they are unable to get your papers or they cannot get you regularized, they don't want to get involved, your bosses don't want to know about it, nothing, nothing, nothing.*[6]

This preference for illegal workers, and the dependence of the worker on their employer, can lead to a vicious circle, with the woman forced into illegality. Vicky,

Table 5.1

SPAIN
DIFFERENT SOCIAL SECURITY ARRANGEMENTS FOR DOMESTIC EMPLOYEES

	GENERAL SCHEME	DOMESTIC SCHEME
Unemployment benefit	yes	no
Leave with pay in accident or sickness	from third day	from 29th day
Retirement pension relative to final wage:		
10 yrs contribution	50%	25%
12 yrs	54%	27%
15 yrs	60%	30%
25 yrs	80%	50%
30 yrs	90%	60%
35 yrs	100%	70%
Supplementary payments to pensioners	yes	no
Early retirement	yes	no
Maximum seniority increment (% of basic wage)	65%	15%
Dismissal notice		
less than 1yr in job	1 month	1 week
more than 1 yr	2-3 months	20 days
Indemnity for justified dismissal	3 weeks wages per year of employment	
Indemnity for improper dismissal	45 days	20 days

Source: Foreign Women in Domestic Service in Madrid, Colectivo Ioe, Spain.

a registered nurse from the Philippines, arrived in Barcelona airport. A person designated by her agency met her and took all her money, $50, in return for a train ticket to the town center. Her employer met her at the station. He told her that she was carrying a fake passport, but that she should not worry, he would fix her papers and settle all her problems.

One month, two, three months passed....... Vicky worked, but was not given her wage, and when she approached her employer, was informed that she was paying in service the amount she owed for him sorting out her documents. Yet she was not allowed to see her papers. In fact, she was not even allowed out of the house, and often kept locked in a room for fear that she might escape. Her days were filled with anxiety and terror, and she thought she would never be free from the clutches of her master. But after six months, she overcame her fear, and seized an opportunity to escape. She is now working without papers, afraid of being caught by the police or by her old employer. When she writes home, she makes no mention of what happened to her, nor of the kind of work she does 'I am ashamed, and my family will be worried.'

The majority of foreign domestic workers in Spain came from the Philippines, with significant numbers from Portugal and Morocco. A broad range of other nationalities, however, is also represented.[7] They come for jobs fixed up in advance by family or friends, or for no particular job at all, but with an idea of working as a domestic, and begin working illegally. They usually work for wealthy employers as live-in servants.

The majority of domestic workers entered Spain after 1975, and the numbers continued to grow until 1986. Figures after that date are difficult to come by because of the increase in unauthorised workers owing to the implementation of the *Ley de la Estranjera* (The Law for Foreigners). This virtually closed Spain as a place for people from the Third World to work legally, and provoked a crackdown on 'illegal immigrants'. It did not, however, decrease the demand for cheap workers, and people continue to enter Spain to work but are not given any form of legal protection. Since the law's introduction, the number of deportations has more than quadrupled from 975 in 1985 to 4,739 in 1989. Street searches and police raids on migrant and immigrant communities have become more and more common, and people can now be deported simply on the grounds of being 'undesirables'. This has created a great deal of apprehension among migrant communities, and specifically has meant that many of those domestics who do not live-in have moved to outlying districts in an effort to avoid police raids.

The Ley de la Estranjera motivated new alliances and groups to spring up within the different migrant communities. In 1989 in Catalonia a federation was set up to devise ways of resisting, and a major demonstration in Madrid was organised with the support of the church, trade unions and human rights groups.

These are small beginnings, but they present the only positive features of an otherwise gloomy picture. Racism is in the ascendant in Spain, as it is everywhere else, and with the new united Europe just around the corner, the real battle for survival for Spain's beleaguered immigrants may only just be beginning.[8]

Italy

Italy shares several characteristics with Spain. Until recently a labour exporting country, it has now become a labour importing nation. The third world immigrant population is small – estimated at some 800,000 at the most; it is not the result of explicit recruitment by the state and employers, rather a less organised response to demand. Like Spain, it is regarded as a 'dangerous' entry point into the EC, and has recently introduced strict immigration control and legislation.

Domestic work is the principal occupation available for migrant women. The workers are from the Philippines, Ethiopia, Cape Verde, Sri Lanka and Thailand. Filipinas constitute the largest national group, followed by Cape Verdeans. In 1980, according to data published by the Ministry of Labour, nearly half the new migrants were employed as domestic servants, and in general domestic workers have been a consistent and significant category of workers entering Italy since it first began attracting labour in 1970. In 1986 and 1987 foreign female domestics constituted more than 50 per cent of the total female domestic workers registered with the National Social Security Institute. This obviously does not include clandestine workers. Domestic workers, and other migrants, are concentrated in the large cities of Rome, Milan, Florence and Turin.

Wages for domestic workers are low – often well below the minimum wage of 730,000 lire (£327) per month – and hours are long: one survey found that nearly 70 per cent of all respondents worked over ten hours a day.[9] This is clearly in breach of the national contract, which is supposed to cover all domestic workers whatever their nationality, and defines working conditions, salaries, benefits for workers and employer/employee obligations. Such inequality is not confined to domestic workers. According to a report on the Saipem oil rig published in 1989 by Comitato di Solidarieta con il Popolo Filippino in Rome, a skilled Filipino welder received only $2.57 per hour whereas a Polish worker doing the same job earned $9 per hour. An English worker earned as much as $12.18 per hour. Italian workers were given four nights rest at home for working 28 days, while Filipino workers doing the same job had no rest days and worked almost 12 hours.[10]

In Italy as elsewhere it is even easier to exploit labour that has been forced into illegality:

> *A prospective employer opts for a migrant woman as cheap labour, having no legal rights owing to her illegal status. The employer can evade labour*
>
> *legislation and fixed minimum wages. The illegal worker has no bargaining power, and the wages are fixed arbitrarily by the employer.*[11]

In Italy as in the Middle East, it is common practice for the employer to hold the domestic's passport.

The situation for domestic workers has worsened in Italy as it has throughout Europe. On 28th February 1990 the 'Martelli Law' was passed, a government decree positing an annual programme for the entry of migrants.

It is important to stress that in an interview given to the daily *La Republica* on 9th June 1990, Martelli clearly implied that from 1991 frontiers would be virtually closed.[12]

While all foreigners living in Italy before December 1989 were regularised, as from 29th June 1990 unauthorised workers could not gain any legal status. Thus the door was effectively closed, even for those who had lived in Italy for many years but whose employers preferred their workers to remain unregistered. This included many domestic workers.

The difficulties for migrants look set to continue. Italy is increasingly dependent on cheap foreign labour, but it is not prepared to acknowledge this. Its birth rate is falling to the extent that one Labour Minister, Carlo Donat Cattin, called on Italians to have more babies 'to keep away armadas of immigrants from the southern shores of the Mediterranean.' Migrants continue to arrive in Italy, unprotected, vulnerable and cheap.

Georgina's Story

Georgina arrived in Rome Central Station to be informed by her recruitment agency that at the moment there was no job for her. She was invited to stay at a pension in the Via della Premule, just for a couple of days, until she had been found a new employer. There were many other Filipinas there in the same situation. The days stretched into weeks during which the stranded young women lived on sardines and bread, board and lodging to be deducted from their salaries. But when would they be given work? Their recruiter was better connected with the world of pimps and prostitutes than the bona fide labour market. As debts mounted with no apparent prospect of work, many women had no option but to work as prostitutes to repay their recruiter and the agency. Those who managed to find work could only do so illegally, and were paid the most meagre wages – 1,000 pesos a month. They too had to turn to prostitution to pay off their debts.

France

At first, France drew most of its legal immigrants from Europe. However, there was a large number of clandestine workers, which were recognised in theory, if not in law, by the government:

Clandestine immigration has its uses, because if we kept to the strict application of international agreements, we would not have enough labour power.[13]

By the 1960s only 23 per cent of immigrants came through the National Office of Immigration, while the remaining 77 per cent were unauthorised.[14]

Immediately after the Second World War it was Algeria which provided a large part of French labour power, both legal and clandestine. However, after independence the Algerian government insisted on certain rights for its emigrants, including accommodation and a return ticket, and France turned to Morocco and Tunisia.

As the number of non-European migrants grew, so did the proportion of women in the migrant labour force. Thirty per cent of these are in 'non-market' services, predominantly domestic work. The proportion of unauthorised female workers in domestic service is even greater. As many as 53.8 per cent of working women who have tourist or expired visas are working as domestics.[15] Unlike their European counterparts, they tend to work as live-in domestics rather than as hourly paid workers coming in every day.

Even for those who are working legally, domestic work is poorly recompensed particularly for those who live-in. The French Labour Code does not set a minimum wage for domestic work, and food and accommodation can be considered as a form of pay. In 1981 43 per cent of all legalised migrant women earned less than 3,000 francs (£314) a month.

There are an estimated 16,000 Filipina domestics in France. Secours-Philippines, an organisation of Filipinas and individual French citizens operating from Paris in much the same way as the Commission for Filipino Migrant Workers does in Britain, is presently undertaking a comprehensive in-depth study of Filipina domestic workers.

Germany

It is now virtually impossible for non-EC nationals to find work legally in Germany. In 1989 new measures were taken to strengthen the immigration law, and since then in general only three month tourist visas have been available. This has serious implications for domestic workers, most of whom are:

> *forced to work illegally with a very low payment, which is neither enough to even repay the money for the air ticket, nor for sending money back home to the Philippines. And since the German police are looking strongly for these foreigners, sooner or later, they are sent back to the Philippines, loaded with thousands of pesos debt they paid for the trip to Germany.*[16]

Although there are many nationalities who work as domestic servants in Germany, research has tended to focus on the situation of Filipinas, who provide a large proportion of the domestic labour and who attracted media attention after several police raids and subsequent deportations.

Filipinas first began working in Germany in the 1960s when they went as nurses and other medical staff. When this was stopped in 1973 the illegal recruitment of Filipinas started. In 1987 there were just over 17,500 Filipinos legally resident in Germany, two thirds of them women. In 1990 the Southeast Asia Information Center estimated there were up to 15,000 Filipinas working illegally in Germany.

Recruiters of Filipina domestic workers charge between £1,700 and £3,400 for jobs in Germany and promise wages greatly inflated from the absolute maximum they could ever hope to earn of £70 a month. Wages of only £17 are more common. The slave wages keep the women in servitude; they stay for years in Germany trying to pay off the recruiters and loan sharks in the Philippines while simultaneously attempting to send money back to their dependants. The longer they stay in illegal work the more difficult it is to change jobs or to try to right their position.

The employers of Filipinas in Germany tend to be families of the US Military Forces. A GI earns about $1,000 a month and there is a huge demand for Filipinas on the grounds that 'the Filipina was the only thing we could afford.' German

Liza's Story

Liza was 32 when her marriage broke down. She was forced to leave her four children, aged between four and nine, with her parents in a small village in Luzon and travel to Manila in search of work. In her anxiety for the children's future she was easy prey to tricksters. A recruiting agency in Manila offered a well-paid job in her own profession, midwifery, in West Germany. They assured her she would easily be able to repay the fees and air fare from her wages. However, at Frankfurt airport she was met by a man who took away her passport, and all her cash. She did not have a work permit, and had permission to stay only for three months. She owed some $5,000. Liza was brought to an American soldier and his wife who promised to pay $200 a month and provide board and lodging for her to work as a baby sitter and domestic helper. The salary was never paid, and it was made very plain to her that she would be 'on her own' should she think of complaining to the police.

The family lived in military married quarters in the Wiesbaden district which had been targeted by German and US military police as a district where as many as 1,000 Filipina maids were working illegally. As the raids got closer Liza's employers removed her bed from the house and allowed her out only after dark. After 18 months they finally disposed of her completely by putting her on a train to Frankfurt. Liza had no money and she could speak no German. She was fortunate in meeting on the train a couple who had themselves been working with migrants, and who could refer her to a support organisation. She is still working in Germany to pay off the debts accruing to her recruitment and travel.[17]

women certainly would not tolerate earning pocket money and duty-free goods from the supermarket. Because they are illegally employed they have no social insurance, and are often turned out if they fall ill. Employers are fined for each illegal working day, and impose severe restrictions to prevent discovery: women must not use the light, nor flush the toilet if the employer is not at home; they are not allowed out, and must take every means to be inconspicuous.

Greece[18]

There are many Greeks living abroad, settled particularly in Europe, North America and Australia. Recently, Greece has become a host country to migrants coming from South East Asia, Africa and Eastern Europe. These new migrants come as domestic workers, hospital aides, and restaurant and hotel workers. Many work on a seasonal basis as agricultural labourers and on construction sites. Greek shipowners have also started to employ large numbers of migrants in their yards and on their ships. Working conditions, pay scales, hours of work and social benefits are far below the standards prevailing in the country, and unacceptable to most Greeks.

There are an estimated 230,000 migrants working in Greece today, with about 30,000 holding work permits. The unauthorised workers are mainly from Philippines, India, Pakistan, Iran, Thailand, Ethiopia and Turkey, and have entered as tourists. There are also many thousands of Albanians, who have to endure increasingly racist attitudes particularly from the Greek police. Greek landlords may refuse to rent homes to non-European foreigners, or charge them much higher rents. Greek shopkeepers mistreat them, sometimes threatening to call the police without reason. SOS Racism have cited cases on Greek boats where African and Asian people are given separate cabins and eat in separate quarters from the white crew. Hospitals and schools are often reluctant to admit foreign workers and their families.

Social activists and trade unionists are increasingly concerned at the lack of measures to protect migrant workers' basic human rights. In one case a domestic worker was accused of stealing and the employer, a Member of Parliament, claimed that he did not know that a work permit was required for her. The woman was deported after being detained for three days without seeing a lawyer. The employer faced no charges. In 1991 19 Filipino midwives working in a Greek hospital were given two days to leave their post. Most of them had worked in the hospital for more than eight years, some as long as fifteen years. The authorities nevertheless refused to give them working and stay permits.[19]

Many migrant workers are employed as domestic helpers, but no work permits are granted for this occupation. The workers must therefore either work illegally, or the prospective employer must prove that a member of their family is in need of nursing care and the worker is then granted a permit as a nursing aide – though in reality she is still a domestic worker. This is a practice known and accepted by the Greek authorities. In order for a visa as a nursing aide to be obtained, the prospective employee must be able to submit appropriate certificates and related work experience; but these are merely a formality and they are not checked.

There is no information as to the numbers and profile of domestic workers in Greece, although they are said to constitute the largest employment sector. There are many reports of abuse, including physical and sexual abuse, excessive working hours, social deprivation and deprivation of food. These problems are aggravated by the attitude of the Greek state towards migration, which has become notably more harsh with the Single European Act, and the increase in numbers of migrants and refugees to Greece.

New legislation includes the creation of a group within the police whose main responsibilities are to track down illegal aliens throughout Greece and to patrol borders. Only after 15 years of legally residing and working in Greece can a person apply for indefinite leave to remain. This is almost impossible, as work permits must be renewed on a yearly basis for maximum of five years. After the fifth year the worker must leave the country within a month or face deportation. Unauthorised workers can be deported within 24 hours. However, this can only be done at the workers' expense or at the expense of the people responsible for bringing them to Greece. Since workers cannot afford to pay their air fare there are many migrants in prisons.

The European Community

The European Economic Community (EEC)[20] was established by the Treaty of Rome in 1957. This provided for the creation of a common market through the progressive elimination of internal customs duties between the member countries – six founder members, since joined by a further six – and the setting up of a common tariff between the EEC and the rest of the world. The UK became a member in 1973.

The Treaty of Rome was amended in 1987 by the Single European Act. This set out to transform the EEC into a single European market by laying down a precise, short-term timetable during which the remaining barriers to economic integration would be abolished. By the close of 1992, there was to be free movement of capital, goods, services and people within the European Communities (EC); the result would be an economic bloc to rival the United States and Japan.

There is little doubt that one of the most contentious areas has been the drive towards geographical mobility within the EC for nationals of the Member States. The real stumbling block is proving to be the method whereby the system is policed; the continental European countries have long become used to a system based on identity cards, with little checking at the internal land frontiers within the Community; whereas the UK, Ireland and, to a lesser extent, Denmark, place their emphasis on immigration controls at ports and airports. This difference in approach has influenced the general tone of EC legislation in such matters, so that EC and British immigration law are not always compatible:

> This is not surprising, because they are based on completely different premises. One of the aims of the EC is to minimise barriers for EC citizens travelling between EC countries for what are defined as economic purposes. On the other hand, the aim of British immigration law is principally to deter economic migration for people who are not EC nationals.[21]

What is not always realised is that discussions, and agreements, between EC countries on matters pertaining to public order, cooperation on policing and immigration, are not handled by the institutions of the EC – the Commission, the Council of Ministers and the European Parliament[22] – but by:

> the beginnings of another state apparatus, made up of ad hoc and secretive bodies and separate inter-governmental arrangements, which reflects the repressive side of European political development and is largely unaccountable and undemocratic in its workings.[23]

The separation of immigration and asylum policies from the mainstream of EC decision-making, and therefore from any democratic accountability to the European Parliament and the national parliaments of Member States, is a cause for concern. It is feared that 'harmonisation' in this area will lead to a 'lowest common denominator' approach to immigration, with governments of the EC countries settling for the most restrictive policies:

> If Germany has 'collection camps' where refugees are detained, so should the rest of Europe. If Germany fingerprints refugees (it has done since 1990), so should the rest of Europe. If Denmark and Italy and Germany and Britain fine airlines who carry refugees without documents, so should the rest of Europe.[24]

The main mechanisms for these inter-governmental discussions are the Trevi group of Ministers, the Ad Hoc Group on Immigration and the Schengen Accord.

The 'policing and security aspects of free movement' are the responsibility of the Trevi group of Ministers, originally established in 1976 to deal with 'terrorism, radicalism, extremism and violence' (hence the name Trevi), and comprising the Home Affairs ministers from the Member States, together with senior police and security chiefs. In Britain it operates under the direction of MI5. From what is known about these secret discussions, the Trevi group has been especially concerned to prevent the entry, and subsequent free circulation, of refugees from third countries using a Member State with 'soft' asylum policies as their entry point. It is through the mechanisms of the Trevi group that EC countries are coordinating the sharing of information on migratory flows and illegal immigration

Fortress Europe: Building the Wall

networks.

The Ad Hoc Group on Immigration meets every six months. Originally set up in October 1986 to 'end abuses to the asylum process,' in 1990 it produced a convention which lays down that responsibility for dealing with applications from asylum-seekers lies with the first country to admit them, whatever the wishes or personal ties, of the individuals concerned. The purpose undoubtedly was to 'persuade' countries liable to be generous with applicants that they would not be able to pass on these unwanted immigrants to others. This was further strengthened at the Maastricht Council, when Member States agreed to common measures on visas, external border controls, conditions of entry for third country nationals and a common information system to monitor and keep out 'undesirables'.

Eight EC countries have already completed the negotiations for an internal market and barrier-free zone between them which goes deeper than the Single Market. The network of so-called 'Schengen' countries was begun by France, Luxembourg, Belgium, the Netherlands and Germany, and now also includes Italy, Spain and Portugal.

The original Schengen Accord (of 1985) committed the participants to abolish barriers between them more fully and faster than the EC as a whole; a Supplementary Agreement (signed in 1990) provides legally binding counter-measures to close the 'security loopholes' arising from the abolition of border controls between the signatories. This covers a host of immigration and police measures as well as internal controls: the criteria and procedures for the issue of visas, the strengthening of external border controls, measures for dealing with asylum-seekers who have come through another Schengen country, penalties for transport operators bringing in undocumented and falsely documented passengers, the setting up of computerised information exchanges on refugees, 'undesirables' and criminals, etc. One of its major weapons is a computerised search apparatus, the Schengen Information System.

The UK has refused to join the Schengen Accord, because it is based on the abolition of internal border controls between signatories. Britain does not trust other member states to prevent access to drug traffickers, terrorists, organised criminals and illegal immigrants, and therefore wants to retain its own frontier controls.

These three inter-governmental groups, unaccountable to member states' democratic processes, are responsible for the EC's immigration policy and legislation and the harmonisation process. Their decisions directly affect the lives of domestic servants, both authorised and unauthorised.

EC immigration policy is thus developing along two main lines. The first is the strengthening of the common external border, the so called 'Fortress Europe'. This means tightening up on visa control, leading perhaps to a common visit visa for entitled non-EC nationals – probably for only three months. This would include all black Commonwealth countries, making it increasingly difficult to make even short visits to see relatives. It means automatic refusal by all EC countries for asylum seekers who have been refused by any other EC country through the so-called Dublin Convention, signed, though not yet ratified by all EC countries. This makes it likely that those countries with more liberal policies for asylum seekers will become more restrictive. Fines on airlines which carry people with no documents have recently been doubled to £2,000.

Those migrants and refugees resident in Europe, unlike EC nationals are not allowed to travel freely. If resident in one EC country they have no right to move to another, but will be subject to the immigration laws of the country they wish to move to. Governments are presently considering ways of checking whether or not people are EC citizens as they travel over borders.

The other development is the increase in so-called 'internal controls': passport checks, and linking immigration to the right to work, to benefits and the health service, effectively creating a second line immigration service and transforming teachers, medical staff and social security officers into its agents. This can only increase pressure on domestic workers to remain with their employers, however abusive the situation. It will also make life even more insecure for those women who have summoned up the courage to run away.

Even those who are European citizens will have their lives made much more difficult:

> For although Trevi is meant to be addressing the problem of terrorists and drug-runners and Schengen the problem of illegal immigrants and refugees as terrorists and drug-runners, a common culture of European racism, which defines all Third World people as immigrants and refugees, and all immigrants and refugees as terrorists and drug-runners, will not be able to tell a citizen from an immigrant or an immigrant from a refugee, let alone one black from another. They all carry their passports on their faces.[25]

It is unclear how these changes will affect foreign domestic workers within the EC generally, and in particular whether those domestic workers travelling with their European employers will enter the UK still under the concession.

1 *Migrant and Refugee Manifesto*, 1989. London: Refugee Forum and Migrant Rights Action Network.
2 The European Community Charter of the Fundamental Social Rights of Workers, adopted in 1989; the UK is not a party to it.
3 Castles Stephen, Booth Heather, Wallace Tina, 1984. *Here for Good: Western Europe's New Ethnic Minorities*, London: Pluto Press.
4 Carr Matthew, 1991. "Racism at the Frontier", *Race and Class*, 32 (3), January-March 1991.
5 Colectivo Ioe 1991. "Foreign Women in Domestic Service in Madrid, Spain". World Employment Programme Working Paper, Geneva: International Labour Office.
6 Colectivo Ioe, ibid.
7 Table 5.2

NATIONALITY OF IMMIGRANTS IN DOMESTIC SERVICE IN CAPITAL REGION, SPAIN		
Country	Number	%
Philippines	353	29.5
Portugal	210	17.5
Morocco	120	10.0
Dominica	81	6.8
Cape Verde	52	4.3
Chile	51	4.2
Colombia	50	4.2
Peru	43	3.6
Argentina	29	2.4
Eq. Guinea	23	1.9
Cuba	21	1.8
El Salvador	20	1.7
Rest of America	67	5.6
Rest of Europe	37	3.1
Rest of Asia	16	1.3
Rest of Africa	13	1.1
Source: Foreign Women in Domestic Service in Madrid, Spain, p.17.		

8 Carr Matthew, ibid.
9 Arena, Gabriella. "Lavoro Femminile de immigrazione: dai Paesi Afro-Asiatici a Roma". In: *Studi Emigrazione*, no 70, Anno XX, Giugno 1983. Quoted in Weinert, Patricia, 1991. "Foreign Female Domestic Workers: Help Wanted!", World Employment Programme Working Paper, Geneva: International Labour Office.
10 Quoted in Pinoy Overseas Chronicle April-May 1989.
11 Weinert, Patricia, ibid.
12 Martiniello, Marco, 1991. "Italy: two perspectives. Racism in paradise?" *Race and Class*, ibid.
13 Jeanneney, J.M., *Les Echos*, 29th March 1966.
14 Lloyd C. and Waters H., 1991. "France: one culture, one people" in *Race and Class*, ibid.
15 Weinert, Patricia, ibid.
16 Filipinas in West Germany – some background information. Leaflet produced by Third World Information Center, Herne.
17 *Die Zeit*, 13th October 1989.
18 Information in this section provided by CFMW international.
19 ASI wrote to the Greek authorities expressing concern at the abrupt dismissal of the women, who did not appear to have any protection under Greek law; and suggesting that their contracts of employment should include specified notices of termination of employment and take account of years of service.
20 The Treaty of Rome created the European Economic Community(EEC); with the Single European Act, this was merged with the Coal and Steel Community (ECSC) and EURATOM to become the European Communities(EC); at the Maastricht Council in 1992, it was decided to change the name again, to European Community.
21 Shutter, Sue, 1992. *Immigration and Nationality Law Handbook*, London: Joint Council for the Welfare of Immigrants.
22 see appendix V for a summary of the functions of the EC's institutions.
23 Bunyan, Tony 1991. "Towards an authoritarian European state", *Race and Class*, ibid.
24 *Statewatch* 2 (2), March-April 1992, London.
25 Sivanandan A., 1991. editorial, *Race and Class*, ibid.

CHAPTER SIX

Not Home Yet:
What Needs to be Done

Migrant domestic workers are found in many parts of the world. There are lessons to be learnt from the way in which two countries in particular have tried to regulate their employment.

Hong Kong

There are more overseas domestic workers in Hong Kong than anywhere else in Asia. The demand took off in the 1970s, when the colony's economy entered a phase of rapid economic growth. Higher levels of education, especially for girls, meant that fewer local people were prepared to undertake domestic work when other job opportunities were available. The number of domestic workers coming from other parts of Asia has been steadily rising since the 1980s, from over 10,000 in 1980 to 89,801 in May 1992.[1]

Filipinas were the among first migrants to go to Hong Kong, and remain by far the largest single group.[2]

By law all domestics have to sign a contract governed by the 1973 Hong Kong Employment Ordinance; this is intended to ensure a minimum standard of employment conditions, and specifies that domestic helpers are entitled to a stated minimum wage, one day off a week, annual paid holidays, the provision of food and accommodation, and free passage to and from Hong Kong. All of these are referred to in the standard employment contract which both parties have to sign. Daily and weekly hours of work however are not stipulated. These contracts run for two years, at the end of which the worker must return home, although this can be waived by the Immigration authorities when both parties have agreed to enter into a new contract. Violations of the contract can be pursued through the legal system. Until 1987, a worker could change her employer after 12 months.

In 1987 however, the Hong Kong Government introduced its New Conditions of Stay for Foreign Domestic Helpers (FDH), otherwise known as the two-week rule. Under this rule, if a domestic leaves her work, for whatever reason, including sexual abuse, or if her employer sacks her, she must leave the colony within 14 days. This rule applies only to domestic workers. It still applies even if an employer withholds her passport, wages and return ticket. If the worker wishes to proceed with a complaint against her employer, she must apply for a visitor's visa. Since cases can take up to a year to get to court, this can mean renewing her visa eight or nine times. Each visa costs money and during this time the migrant is not allowed to work.

As abuse takes place mainly in a domestic environment, it can be difficult to prove; if many workers are reluctant to make formal complaints, even less can they afford the lengthy legal process and the total lack of income which comes with it. The Asian Domestic Workers Union, founded in January 1989, has been overwhelmed by the number of grievances from members. The Hong Kong Council of Women in 1991 stated publicly its belief that the numbers of workers sent home as documented by the Mission for Filipino Migrant Workers, and the cases known to solicitors, represented 'just the tip of the iceberg'.[3] Thus the effect of the two-week rule is to deprive overseas domestics of the power to terminate a contract.

In August 1991, the Asian Migrant Centre in Hong Kong published the results of an investigation into the general situation of overseas domestic workers in the colony, based on interviews with over 2,000 workers.

Table 6.1
FOREIGN DOMESTIC WORKERS IN HONG-KONG:
- nearly half are aged between 25 and 34; many, especially the Filipinas, have degrees and diplomas;
- 93 per cent do household duties, 45 per cent take care of children and the elderly, 8 per cent also have to work in other households or businesses;
- over 80 per cent work 14 or more hours a day, with 45 per cent of Indians and 36 per cent of Sri Lankans working over 16 hours a day;
- most workers receive the salaries specified in their contracts, and sometimes more, but underpayment is the rule where Indian and Sri Lankan domestics are concerned;
- almost half the employing families have double earners and 83 per cent have at least one child;
- 62 per cent of the employers are Chinese, and 30 per cent are British and Westerners;
- scolding is common, often with threats of termination and repatriation, with Indians reporting the most abuse;
- the highest incidence of physical abuse is suffered by Sri Lankans, reported by 13 per cent of them.

Source: Asian Migrant Centre survey, 1991

This information is illuminating in that it shows that a contract of itself, while clearly helpful, is not enough to prevent abuse; it also seems to indicate that the more educated workers, those more likely to know their rights and perhaps be willing to stand up for them, are also those less likely to suffer exploitation. Ultimately, however, the contracts have become in effect unenforceable under the two-week rule.[4]

Canada

The 1960s saw the start of the demand for maids in Canada, and at that time West Indians met the need. At that time, immigration seemed the obvious answer and bilateral agreements were reached with a number of countries. Once in Canada, the migrants had the right to freedom of movement and the right to change jobs. Frequently however maids changed out of domestic work. New regulations were introduced in 1971.

The federal government decided to grant temporary entry only and, in effect, the domestics found themselves tied to one employer. By the mid-70s, the position was causing official concern. The conditions for abuse were there, and some employers were taking advantage of their position. In addition, the authorities realised that they had no real method of policing to make sure that exploitation did not happen as there was no specific legislation covering domestic workers.

In 1981, Canada introduced a Foreign Domestic Movement Program. This allows workers giving 'live-in care', including domestics, the right to enter to work for a specific employer with a one-year permit; this can be extended for up to three years, and after two years, the worker may apply for permanent resident status. Workers can only come in under this programme if government officials have agreed that the employers need a live-in carer, and the employers sign a contract specifying the terms: duties, hours, time off and wages, all of which are governed by legislation. At the end of the first year of the contract, the immigration authorities have a discretionary power to interview the worker.

This contract system has gone some way to meeting the requirement of the employer for a stable worker, and that of the worker for the right to change employer and to be free of exploitation. In particular, workers are permitted to change jobs, but they must first apply for a new employment authorisation. Employers found to be abusing the contract terms are refused permission to hire foreign domestics again.

Being openly recognised as a possible route to permanent residence, the government requires the workers to speak either French or English and to meet certain education, health and work experience criteria.

Recent figures show that, in the ten years since the start of the programme, the number of 'live-in carers' entering Canada has grown from 3,500 to 7,260 in 1991. The Philippines, which provided 15 per cent of participants in 1981, now account for 68 per cent; and workers from the Caribbean, originally 15 per cent of participants, represent only 4.7 per cent of the total.[5]

In 1992, modifications were made to the scheme, now rechristened the 'Live-in Caregiver Program'. Still described as "designed to meet a labour market shortage," the government says "the changes strike a balance between the needs of the employer and those of the live-in caregiver".[6] In particular, the worker no longer needs a release letter to change employer; on the other hand, the education level on entry has been made more stringent, with the applicant having to demonstrate the equivalent of Canadian grade 12 (A-level in the UK).

The Canadian system does not of itself prevent abuse and exploitation. But the worker's ability to change employer (while remaining in the same category of work) and to seek redress in the courts go a long way to regulating the situation. Both are absent when it comes to overseas domestic workers in Britain.

Issues requiring further investigation

In the course of the research undertaken for this book a number of issues have come to light which are beyond the immediate scope of this report, yet require investigation if the situation of migrant domestic workers in Britain and elsewhere in Europe is to be improved.

The first is that, as touched on in the stories told in the previous pages, overseas domestic workers in Britain come from many parts of the world. Both Kalayaan and the Commission for Filipino Migrant Workers (CFMW) have become known in the past few years as organisations willing and able to help overseas domestic workers in difficulty, with the result that local councils, churches, advice agencies and individuals contact them for assistance. They now have on their files cases involving women from India, Sri Lanka and elsewhere in Asia, as well as women from different parts of Africa, from the Caribbean and from Latin America.

When it comes to women from Africa, a number are being declared as members of the employer's family; while in some cases this may well be true, they are being brought in as domestic servants. The abuse is often exacerbated by the fact that the young domestic workers may be only partially literate – indeed their families have sometimes been promised that the young women will receive an education in the UK. Furthermore, in one case which came to court in early 1993, an employer was found guilty of facilitating an illegal entry, bringing in a young woman using the passport of her previous domestic servant who had run away to escape abuse.

The point at issue is that, while the focus of this report has been on overseas domestic workers who have entered the United Kingdom under the concession, it is clear that there are also a number of other women who have been brought into the UK as domestic workers and who are suffering under conditions akin to slavery. Some of these, it appears, may be additionally disadvantaged because the fraud of those bringing them in means that their status has been illegal from the start. This situation needs to be addressed. In particular, as a matter of justice, the employee should not be penalised because of an offence committed by the employer.

The second issue which, in our view, requires further consideration, is the Europe-wide situation of migrant domestic workers. Our research has only touched on the problem, but even the brief account in the previous chapter indicates that all is not well, and that matters may get worse with developments in the EC.

The most urgent requirement here is for facts, to seek to establish the measure of the problem. As indicated, there are Filipino organisations in other EC countries; and there has been the beginning of European-level campaigning by Filipino and African groups. We would urge as a matter of urgency that research be undertaken into this, and would suggest that the Commission of the European Communities, and indeed the European Parliament, should take a lead in such a venture.

The third issue brings us back to the situation in the United Kingdom. Our investigations have indicated that little attention is being paid to the overall situation faced by domestic workers generally.

There is no statutory requirement in UK employment law for a written contract (for anyone) other than an obligation on the employer to give a written statement to the employee with information on the pay, the terms and conditions, no later than 13 weeks after the start of the period of employment. It is this statement – or its absence – which forms the basis of any referral to an Industrial Tribunal.

Kalayaan, together with the Service Workers Action and Advisory Project (SWAAP), has drawn up a model contract of employment for domestic workers to use as a basis for negotiations with potential employers. This is given by Kalayaan and CFMW to overseas domestics who come to them for advice (reproduced at Appendix VI). The Transport & General Workers Union (TGWU) has also issued an advice leaflet specifically for overseas domestic workers, encouraging them to join the union. More needs to be done, and we would urge organisations and trade unions working in fields involving low-paid workers to turn their attention to the situation of domestic workers, particularly live-in domestics, with a view to producing and promoting guidelines to good practice by employers, and seeking to have them used by Industrial Tribunals.

Recommendations for action in the UK

Our recommendations take as a starting point two principles which have been accepted by all sides. These are:

- that the practice of admitting domestic workers should be continued, and
- that the main problem is to prevent the abuse of domestic workers.

The Home Office has emphasised that it seeks a solution consistent with current immigration practice, and we believe that our recommendations fulfil this criterion. We take as our starting point the fact that the permission to enter given to overseas domestic workers is already a concession, and that there is therefore no reason why this concession should not be modified.

To date, the Home Office, as is clear from the letter of 25th January 1993 to ASI from the Immigration and Nationality Department (reproduced at Appendix IV), continues to lay stress on the fact that the concession is intended to overcome the difficulties of employers; and that, while 'sympathetic to the argument that overseas domestics are more vulnerable to exploitation than other groups of workers', the new leaflet and related arrangements meet the concerns expressed. This is far from the case.

The solution lies in changes which achieve four main goals, outlined below:

1. Right to recognition as workers

Under the current work permit scheme, overseas domestic workers are not like workers in other sectors entering the United Kingdom with work permits. They come in under a 'concession' outside the Immigration Rules – a concession which is openly intended to assist their employers by not depriving them of their accustomed domestic help.

The position of the Home Office is that it is not prepared to reintroduce work permits for the domestic worker category. But the concession is already an attempt to square this circle, and one which, in the view of many, is at present weighed against the employee.

Domestic work is subject to low pay and poor conditions; whether British or immigrant, domestic workers in this country are among the least protected members of the workforce; by depriving overseas domestic workers of the status of workers, the Home Office is exacerbating their plight.

We therefore urge that:

overseas domestic workers should have a status which recognises that they are workers.

2. Right to transfer employers

Given that, by the very nature of the concession, domestic servants accompanying their employers arriving from abroad are acknowledged as working, to this extent granting them the facility to transfer employment would be consistent with the practice as applied to other overseas workers in the UK.

Indeed, the ability to change employers would of itself act as a powerful deterrent to abusive employers.

Additionally, in cases where domestic workers who have been victims of abuse wish to seek compensation, it is disingenuous to pretend that they can support themselves without working while the complaint is pursued – especially since, as we have described, they will often have been denied their wages.

We therefore urge that:

overseas domestic workers be allowed to change employers within the same category of employment.

3. Right to settle after four years

It is a standard provision of work permits to overseas workers that they be allowed to settle in this country after four years in the category of work for which the work permit was granted. Indeed under the Immigration Rules Concession as presently constituted the Government grants this right to overseas domestic workers too – if they stay for the whole of that period with their original employer.

In this form this is less a 'right' than yet another means of tying the worker to their employers, since it cannot be exercised independently and is lost immediately the worker leaves the employer. Moreover it can be revoked by the employer simply by discharging the worker at any time within the four years – a 'right', in other words, which for four years is surrendered to employers to dispense or withdraw, or threaten to withdraw, at whim.

We therefore urge that:

the Government give overseas domestic workers the right to settle in this country after four years of work within their category irrespective of whether they transferred to another employer.

4. One-off right to regularise immigration status.

We hope that the Government will listen to our recommendations for action and introduce measures to discourage abuse in the future. We suggest however, that the Government has a moral responsibility towards those already driven underground by a combination of unbearable abuse – which provoked them into running away – and the inflexibility of the authorities to-date.

We would urge that:

those overseas domestic workers who have already left their employers and are now overstayers should have their immigration status regularised.

In short, we ask that overseas domestic workers be recognised as workers with rights, and that in particular this must include the right to change employers within their category of work and the right to settle in the country after four years of such work; and that the legal status of those who have fled their employers and are now overstayers be regularised. These measures would both prevent future abuse and redress some of the harms of our present abuse-ridden system.

We further ask the Government to ensure that, once it has instituted these changes, the overseas domestic workers and above all their employers be made aware of their rights and obligations under law.

Repeating calls for action which Anti-Slavery International and Kalayaan have consistently urged on the Government since 1987, and which have been endorsed by MP's, peers, other leading public figures and the many thousands who have written letters and signed petitions indicating their support, we publish this book as a call for change now.

1 Foreign Domestic Helpers in Hong Kong: Assistance Manual, 1992. Hong Kong: Asian Migrant Centre.
2 The official figures for foreign domestic workers in Hong Kong by nationality in 1991 are:

Nationality	Number of Workers
Burmese	72
Filipina	65,924
Indian	842
Indonesian	1,215
Malaysian	46
Nepali	34
Pakistani	51
Singaporean	9
Sri Lankan	338
Thai	4,516

Source: *Asian Migrant Forum*, 1991-1992, Issues 3 & 4.

3 in a petition to the Governor.
4 On 20th April 1987, United Filipinos in Hong Kong, an alliance of 14 migrant organisations, wrote to the then Governor, Sir David Wilson, pointing out that the new rules '*virtually make modern-day slaves of us*'; in 1991, ASI in the second of two submissions on migrant domestic workers to the UN Working Group on Contemporary Forms of Slavery, highlighted the effect of the two-week rule and called for its replacement with legislation conforming to acceptable standards of human rights; ASI also asked that the contracts include the number of hours to be worked each day (text of submission obtainable from ASI).
5 Government Press Release announcing the new Live-in Caregiver Program, 27th April 1992, Minister of Employment and immigration, Canada.
6 Ibid.
7 letter from the Immigration and Nationality Department, Home Office, to ASI, 25th January 1993; full text at Appendix IV.

APPENDIX I

The Legal Status of Overseas Domestic Workers in the United Kingdom

Introduction
This appendix is intended to provide a brief introduction to the legal status of overseas domestic workers in the United Kingdom in relation to immigration control, the legal redress of abuse and European texts.

Each area of law is extremely complex with a body of relevant case law as well as statutory provisions that fall outside the scope of these pages. Reliable legal advice needs to be sought by domestic workers – and also those befriending them – as soon as possible after escaping from their employers. However, the anomalous position of domestic workers and the ever present risk of deportation will, in reality, prevent many workers from seeking legal redress.

1. Immigration Control

The Immigration Act 1971 and the Immigration Act 1988 are the two main statutes in the area of immigration law. The 1971 Immigration Act gives wide powers to the Home Secretary with regard to immigration:

> *s.1(4) The rules laid down by the Secretary of State as to the practice to be followed in the administration of this Act for regulating the entry into and stay in the UK of persons not having the right of abode shall include provisions for admitting (in such cases and subject to such restrictions as may be provided by the rules, and subject or not to conditions as to length of stay or otherwise) persons coming for the purpose of taking employment, or for purposes of study, or as visitors, or as dependents of persons lawfully in or entering the UK.*

This section provides for broad areas in which the Home Secretary can administer Immigration Rules. The Immigration Rules although not strictly law are of the utmost importance. The present Rules are contained in HC 251 1990 as amended. The powers that control decisions surrounding entry, stay or deportation come from the Immigration Act itself and not the Rules. This is an important consideration because this allows a departure from the Rules in favour of the immigrant (most clearly seen in the case of the domestic worker). The departure will not thus be in breach of the law as it is a prerogative discretion. Section 3(2) of the 1971 Act empowers the Home Secretary to lay down these Rules:

> *s.3(2) The Secretary of State shall from time to time (and as soon as maybe) lay before Parliament statements of the rules, or of any changes in the rules, laid down by him as to the practice to be followed by him in the administration of this Act for regulating the entry into and stay in the UK of persons required by this Act to have leave to enter, including any rules as to the period for which leave is to be given and the conditions to be attached in different circumstances; and s.1(4) above shall not be taken to require uniform provision to be made by the rules as regards admission of a person for a purpose or capacity specified in s.1(4).*

A statement of the Rules or of changes in the Rules is laid before Parliament, and if not disapproved within 40 days the Rules are authorised.

The above details the broad base from which the Home Secretary can act with regards to immigration. The legislation and the Rules give the Home Secretary formidable legal powers in this area.

Entry Rules

Para. 14-17 of the Immigration Rules 1990 HC 251 deal with the requirements relating to entry clearance; the latter may take the form of a visa, a letter of consent, or an entry clearance certificate.

Diplomatic Missions

Domestic servants coming to the country with members of the staffs of diplomatic or consular missions are specifically mentioned in the Immigrations Rules (HC 251 40(a)). They are permitted to enter the UK without work permits under the permit free scheme subject to their having the proper entry clearance. They are admitted for a period of not more than 12 months extendable on application.

In addition, the Immigration Acts 1971 and 1988 grant exemption from control to members of diplomatic missions (within the meaning of the Diplomatic Privileges Act 1964) with respect to the provisions of the Immigration Act; the person must be a member of the mission itself to gain exemption. Very few domestic workers are members of a mission and therefore exempt from immigration control.

The 'concession'

Domestic servants who are accompanying their employers to the UK are admitted outside the Immigration Rules under a concession to their employers which first appeared in 1980 after work permits for this category were phased out. The concession allows the employer to bring a category of worker to the UK who would normally not be admitted. As this has operated outside the Rules it has led to substantial confusion. On some occasions domestic workers are given leave to enter as a visitor; this is despite the fact that the Immigration Rules (HC 251 (22)) state that a visitor is to be refused entry if the Immigration Officer believes that the real purpose of the visit is to take employment. This was the position in the case of Amelia Mendoza v Secretary of State for the Home Department [(1992) Imm AR 122]. It is clear that the Officer knows that the domestic servant is coming to work.

The period of leave to enter given to the domestic worker is usually six months, employment prohibited, the maximum a visitor can have. If the worker is admitted as a visitor, the Rules do not permit a change of worker status. Also if s/he changes employment any variation of leave will be referred to the Department of Employment, who will not normally allow this change. The conditions under which leave to enter was granted have changed and as such it would be treated as an application for a work permit. A noteworthy point is that although officially workers with work permits are not allowed to change employment, in practice they are allowed to change within their 'category of employment'. The Home Office claim that they cannot allow domestic workers to change employer within their category of employment because no other foreign worker is allowed to do this. Given the above mentioned practice this claim can be seen to be somewhat flawed. The effect of this situation is that a worker is tied to a particular employer.

The new measures

In May 1991 new measures were introduced by the Home Office concerning the domestic worker concession. These are summarised as follows:

* All domestic workers would have to be at least 17 and to have worked 12 months for their employers if they were visiting the UK and 24 months if their employers intended to remain in the UK.

* Domestic workers would need prior entry clearance, even if they came from countries where there is not normally any visa requirement.

* Domestic workers would have to be interviewed by an entry clearance officer overseas before coming to the UK.

* Domestic workers would be issued with a new explanatory leaflet setting out their rights and where to get help if needed. This would also be given to the employer.

These measures have been criticised on a number of fronts, as follows:

(1) How can a previous employment be proved?
(2) It is widely felt that a leaflet alone cannot prevent these abuses.
(3) The content of the leaflet is questionable as it does not set out the criminal

offences and sanctions that can be used against an abusing employer. It does not set out the civil liabilities and responsibilities of employers. It does not explain that the employer is not permitted to confiscate the worker's passport. The only person specifically threatened with prosecution in the leaflet is the domestic worker who overstays. An impediment to the willingness of domestic workers to enforce their rights is the fear of the immigration consequences of enforcement. There is no mention of the possibility of remaining in the UK to enforce these rights.

Variation of leave to remain

Section 3 of the Immigration Act 1971 deals with the powers to vary leave, they are also covered in para.94 145 HC 251.

A domestic worker, with the same employer who wishes to remain for a longer period than the initial leave, can apply to the Home Office. The application should include a letter setting out the circumstances in which leave to remain is required, and also a passport or travel document. After four years with the same employer the domestic servant under the concession is given indefinite leave to remain. Ironically, domestic workers of diplomats under the permit free scheme qualify for indefinite leave after ten years. It is not surprising to discover that employers often dismiss the worker before this period arises.

Domestic workers who run away and/or overstay

Problems occur if the domestic servant runs away from the employer or becomes an overstayer. In R v Secretary of State for the Home Department ex parte Dordas [(1992) Imm AR 99] a domestic servant had run away because of the abuse she had received from her employers. The immigration authorities tried to claim that this action could amount to illegal entry by deception under ss.26(1)(c) and 33(1) of the 1971 Act. They based their case on the premise that before she came to the UK she had intended to run away, and the fact that she had not represented this amounted to a deception. This argument failed as the judge could not accept that non disclosure could amount to a representation. Kennedy J. in this case recognised domestic servants' lack of participation in being brought to the UK. He said (at p.101) she:

> took very little part in the preparations that were being made in Kuwait, in particular in the British Embassy, as to what was going to take place.

One may wonder about the entry clearance procedures; Kennedy J. says (at p.101):

> although she did sign an entry clearance form she did so in blank and it was filled in by the secretary or the embassy staff with what were considered to be the appropriate answers.

Another problem occurs if the domestic worker overstays. This is a criminal law offence and is governed by s.24(1)(b) of the 1971 Act; a person is liable:

> *if, having only a limited leave to enter or remain in the UK, he knowingly either-*
> *(i) remains beyond the time limited by leave; or*
> *(ii) fails to observe a condition of the leave.*

This is different from s.3(5) of the 1971 Act in that it is an actual criminal law offence; s.3(5)(a) merely lays out the administrative powers of a deportation which are available to the Secretary of State:

> *if, having only a limited leave to enter or remain, he does not observe a condition attached to the leave or remains beyond the time limited by leave.*

These administrative powers are so strict and the appeal rights against them so limited that prosecutions under s.24(1)(b) are rarely pursued.

Rights of appeal

Under Section 14(1) of the 1971 Act an in time application to vary leave attracts a right of appeal to an adjudicator on refusal. The chances of success vary with the particular circumstances of the case but there is now unfortunately case law covering most of the common scenarios in which a domestic worker admitted as a visitor seeks to transfer employment. Under s.15(1) of the 1971 Act a person may appeal to an adjudicator against a decision to deport. The Immigration Act 1988 s.5(1)(a) severely restricts the right to appeal against a decision to deport for appellants who have been in the UK less than seven years at the time that the decision to deport was made. For that group an appeal can generally only be launched if there is in law no power to make the deportation order. As one can imagine this will rarely be the case.

Judicial review may be available in certain limited circumstances: illegality, irrationality and procedural impropriety.

The actual immigration status of domestic workers is in a dangerously confused state. Although admitted with the full knowledge that they will be in employment, they are often admitted on a visitor's stamp.

2. Redress through UK Criminal and Civil Courts

Adequate and practically enforceable legal protection is vital if anything is to be done about the abuses which domestic servants suffer. The potential legal protection open to the domestic worker will be considered in the areas of criminal law, civil litigation and employment law.

Criminal Law

The purpose of a criminal prosecution is to punish the wrongdoer. Procedurally the victim of a crime complains to the police who investigate, arrest and then charge the perpetrator if they deem the complaint to be capable of proof to the high standard required by the criminal law.

It has to be said at the outset that prosecutions of employers are rare, both because of the understandable reluctance of domestic workers to initiate them and also because there are often evidential problems that make the police reluctant to act, notably the isolation of the victim and difficulty in finding reliable witnesses to corroborate his/her testimony.

Charges which may be brought against abusing employers in appropriate circumstances are:

(i) Sexual Offences

Criminal law offences under the Sexual Offences Act 1956 will be relevant in cases where sexual assault is involved. Section 14(1) makes an indecent assault on a woman an offence. The essential requirements of an assault are that the defendant must have either intentionally or recklessly inflicted unlawful personal violence on the victim or intentionally or recklessly caused the victim to apprehend the immediate infliction of such violence. The question of 'indecent' is a matter of fact for a jury.

Section1(1) of the Sexual Offences (Amendment) Act 1976 deals with the offence of rape.

(ii) Offences of Violence

For most crimes of violence without a sexual element the Offences Against the Persons Act 1862 will be relevant; the standard offences in decreasing order of severity are as follows:

s.18 covers unlawful and malicious wounding with or without a weapon, where it is possible to prove that it was accompanied by an intention to do grievous bodily harm to another person;

s.20 also covers unlawful and malicious wounding causing grievous bodily harm with or without a weapon; in the case of s.20 it is necessary to prove that a person intended an assault, but not necessarily to cause grievous bodily harm;

s.47 deals with the offence of an assault which occasions actual bodily harm; the definition of actual bodily harm extends to any injury, for instance it is not necessary to puncture the skin to cause actual bodily harm, however medical evidence to substantiate that there was some sort of injury is usually necessary.

There is a further offence of common assault contrary to s.39 Criminal Justice Act 1988; this is a minor offence and it is not necessary to show more than the intentional threat of unwanted physical contact; although in practice it is unlikely that there will be a criminal charge unless there has been some physical contact such as a kick or slap.

(iii) Other Offences
There are other offences remaining on the statute book which are theoretically relevant to the forms of abuse frequently experienced by domestic workers (eg wilfully and without lawful excuse to refuse or neglect to provide sufficient food, clothing or lodgings for servants). Experience suggests that the police and Crown Prosecution Service (CPS) are unlikely to base prosecutions on such archaic criminal law. Private prosecutions are theoretically possible without the support of the police or CPS, but Legal Aid funds are not available and the expense and evidential difficulties combine to make this not a viable form of legal redress for domestic workers.

(iv) Criminal Injuries Compensation Board
In the event of any of these crimes, as laid out above, a claim may be made for compensation to the Criminal Injuries Compensation Board (CICB). This may be necessary if for example the employer has left the jurisdiction of the court. It has to be claimed within three years of the incident which caused the injury, and an award will only be made where the victim of the crime has co-operated with the police, so a crime must be reported at the latest when the CICB claim is made and normally before that.

(v) Diplomatic Immunity
Another relevant consideration here is the immunity from criminal law given to diplomats. This sprung from the Vienna Convention on Diplomatic Relations and was enacted here by the Diplomatic Provisions Act 1964. Diplomatic staff and the Heads of missions are immune from both criminal and civil actions. Members of the administration and technical staff as well as their household members have immunity from the criminal law. Immunity from civil actions is only afforded if they are acting in the course of their duties (Diplomatic Privileges Act 1964 Sch.1 Art.37 Para.2). Since to act unlawfully against a worker cannot be in the course of their duties, a civil action is therefore possible.

Claiming Compensation through the Civil Courts
The UK Civil Courts do not seek to punish wrongdoers, but to compensate the victims of wrong doing. This is the only area where domestic workers can claim damages for breach of contract such as non payment of wages and other forms of abuse.

(i) False Imprisonment
This is also an offence against the criminal law, but rarely prosecuted. False imprisonment is where a person is deprived of liberty for any period of time, however short, without lawful cause. Case law suggests that there can be

psychological imprisonment not involving the use of actual force or direct physical contact and it has been held by the Courts that where a worker is confined to a house that will constitute false imprisonment.

Where a domestic worker is not physically locked in, but is too frightened to leave the house; even in the not uncommon situation where she accompanies children to a park chaperoned by other members of the household, she may still be able to argue that she has been falsely imprisoned. In those circumstances it will depend to what extent she was psychologically imprisoned and unable to exercise any reasonable means of escape.

(ii) Assault and Battery

This is similar to common assault described above. To claim compensation for assault it is theoretically enough to show that a person has been subjected to an immediate threat of unwanted physical contact. But in reality it will only be worthwhile suing for assault and battery if some sort of injury has been sustained, otherwise the damages would be too minimal to justify an action.

(iii) Intimidation

This would arise where an employer intentionally coerces a worker by the use of threat or actual unlawful treatment, into doing or not doing something which is to the detriment of that worker. For instance, where threats of violent chastisement are used to force a worker to work excessive hours or to go without adequate food the tort (wrongful act) of intimidation could be used.

(iv) Breach of Contract

The contract of employment can be written or oral. As well as express terms there will also be terms implied at common law (these would be universal) and terms implied using the 'officious bystander' test; this is basically a test which asks what the ordinary, reasonable person would think was so obvious that it did not have to be put down in the contract. These terms apply specifically to the individual's contract. The common law terms will be fundamental and impose the following:

* provision of a safe working environment;
* the giving of only lawful and reasonable orders;
* to maintain a relationship of mutual trust and confidence;
* payment of reasonable remuneration.

One can only guess at terms that would be implied by the 'officious bystander' test, but they might include the provision of enough food and reasonable time off.

If any of the above terms are breached then the worker will be entitled to treat the contract as terminated. A claim for damages could then be made so long as there is no illegality in the contract of employment. This can occur if the worker has remained in the UK after the period of leave which had been granted or if the worker has been allowed into the country as a visitor and has secured employment contrary to the conditions of entry.

Non payment of wages can be recovered through the provisions of Part 1 of the Wages Act 1986; this will involve an Industrial Tribunal:

> *s.1(1) An employer shall not make any deduction from any wages of any worker employed by him unless the deduction satisfies one of the following conditions:*
>
>> *(a) it is required or authorised to be made by virtue of any statutory provision or any relevant provision of the worker's contract;*
>>
>> *(b) the worker has previously signified in writing his agreement or consent to the making of it.*

At least one such claim has been brought successfully against an employer of a domestic worker for non payment of wages. There are a number of advantages to bringing a claim to an Industrial Tribunal: costs are very rarely awarded if a claim is unsuccessful; an ACAS conciliation officer will be despatched to try to reach a settlement; and employers tend to settle at this stage.

(v) Slavery

Under the Slavery Abolition Act of 1833, slaves brought to England were to be considered free. There could be contradictions between the UK law on slavery and the UN Conventions - ratified by the UK - which, to our knowledge, have not been tested either in the UK or in European Courts.

There has been one attempt to use the 1833 Slavery Abolition Act to prevent an escaped domestic worker from being deported. On 15th November 1991, lawyers for Mahesh Kumari Rai argued in the High Court that Mahesh had not been a free agent during her residence with her employers and therefore qualified as an escaped slave who was entitled to residence.

Mr Justice Popplewell described the slavery argument as 'interesting', but said that it was not relevant to her case against deportation, which raised no point in law. Despite further appeals, Mahesh was finally deported: the campaign on her behalf is described in Chapter 4.

The relevance of the 19th century slavery laws to the position of domestic workers brought into the UK therefore has yet to be fully tested before the Courts.

The problem with these statutes is that it would appear that a domestic servant no longer has slave status after leaving the employer. In addition, the contractual relationship, which is indicated by the presence of a contract, could suggest that the employee does not have the formal status of a slave.

The United Nations Supplementary Convention on the Abolition of Slavery, the Slave Trade, and Institutions and Practices Similar to Slavery (1956) includes debt bondage as a form of slavery. It is not unusual for people in a situation of debt bondage to have contracts, and under the UN Convention it is in practice the various aspects of the contract which determine whether a person is in a situation of slavery.

3. European Texts

The European Convention on Human Rights

The European Convention on Human Rights (1950) is one of the earliest and most important instruments of the Council of Europe. It covers everyone who is specifically within the jurisdiction of the courts. Article 4 specifically mentions freedom from slavery or servitude, and from forced or compulsory labour. The problem lies with the impracticability of enforcement for the domestic worker, who must have exhausted all domestic remedies before making a claim. Even then the application may be declared 'incompatible' with the Convention.

The European Social Charter

The European Social Charter (1961) is also an instrument of the Council of Europe, intended to complement the European Convention. It sets out targets for moving towards improved working conditions, and articles 18 & 19 deal specifically with migrant workers. However, only migrant workers who are nationals of a Contracting Party are covered by these articles.

The Treaty of Rome

The European Economic Community (EEC) provided for the free movement of workers in articles 48 & 49 of its founding document, the Treaty of Rome. The matter has since been dealt with extensively by the EC. But, in order to qualify for the protection extended by the Treaty and subsequent instruments, the worker has to be a national of a Member state.

The Community Charter of the Fundamental Social Rights of Workers

The Community Charter of the Fundamental Social Rights of Workers (1989) was adopted (minus the UK) to pave the way for new social legislation arising from the single market programme. It mentions in its Preamble:

> *Whereas it is for the Member states to guarantee that workers from non member countries and members of their families who are legally resident in a Member state of the EC are able to enjoy as regards their living and working conditions treatment comparable to that enjoyed by workers who are nationals of the Member state concerned.*

Whereas inspiration should be drawn from the conventions of the ILO and from the European Social Charter of the Council of Europe.

Section 1 deals with the freedom of movement of EC nationals; s.4 grants every individual the freedom to choose and engage in an occupation; s.5 deals with fair remuneration for work undertaken; s.8 specifies that every worker must enjoy satisfactory health and safety conditions at work. These rights are all denied to the domestic worker who is tied to the one employer.

The 'Communication from the Commission concerning its action programme relating to the implementation of the Community Charter of the Fundamental Social Rights of Workers' (COM (89) 568 Final) states that:

> *3 Improvement of living and working conditions.*
>
> *Furthermore, in the Commission's view even if free movement only applies to the workers of the Community and their families, the fact cannot be overlooked that there are at present several million non Community workers in the Community. The Commission intends to submit a memorandum on this subject, which should be a subject of wide ranging debate within the circles concerned.*

This debate is presumably still going on.

European Directive on a form of proof of the employment relationship

A recent EC Directive 'On a form of proof of an employment relationship' (OJ 1991 C24/3) is relevant to the status of domestic workers:

> *Article 1*
>
> *1. This directive applies to any employment relationship which is subject to the legislation in force in a Member state.*

Article 2(1) places a duty on an employer to provide the worker with a written declaration, which should contain (Art.2(2)) an identification of the parties, the place of work, a description of the job and the category of employment, duration of the employment relationship, working time and paid leave, remuneration and method of payment. By Art.2(3) the employer must give written notification of any changes in the terms of employment. Art.3 maintains that none of this is necessary if there is a contract of employment.

Basically this Directive is trying to make sure that in every employment relationship there is actual proof of the terms and conditions involved. The Directive is due to be implemented in the UK during 1993. The proof of terms and conditions of employment would be very useful in a legal action by a domestic worker.

Conclusion
There are a number of areas of the law that offer protection to the domestic worker. They must be viewed in the context of the insecure position of the worker, who is tied to the one employer, and under the permanent threat of deportation. This must be borne in mind in any discussion of legal rights and their enforcement.

APPENDIX II

ANTI-SLAVERY SOCIETY

REPORT TO THE WORKING GROUP ON CONTEMPORARY FORMS OF SLAVERY, 1990

DOMESTIC WORKERS

When the High Court in London awarded damages of £300,000 to Laxmi Swami last December (1989), justice was seen to be done. But the case , because of its prominence, also illuminated the secret world of domestic slavery.

Laxmi Swami, a poor village woman from south India, originally worked for £15 a week in Kuwait for two members of the Emir's family, Sheika Faria al Sabah and Sheika Samiya. The job of maid had been found for her by an Indian labour recruiter. She was eventually bought to London by the princesses and stayed with them in a mansion in Bayswater, one of London's more affluent districts. There, for four years, she lived what has been described as a life of hell.

She was deprived of food, frequently had only two hours of sleep a night, and her 'bedroom' was the floor outside the locked kitchen. She was never allowed out, received no wages and was whipped every day. She is scarred for life. On one occasion the two princesses forcibly removed her two gold teeth. Her passport was also taken from her.

Immediately after the High Court judgement Mrs Swami said:

> Once these rich people come to Britain and take your passport, they see you as their slave.

The Anti-Slavery Society, which is at the beginning of its investigation into the plight of overseas domestic workers, regards that statement as an encapsulation of the unavoidable truth.

The Society is aware that domestic slavery is not confined to Britain and instances of it, in varying degrees, may be found in Middle Eastern states, in Hong Kong, in North America and in member states of the EC.

For the purpose of this submission the Society will focus on the United Kingdom.

It will also exclude the drudgery and exploitation of domestic workers, many of whom are girl children, by their fellow nationals in their home countries.

The 1971 Immigration Act gives the Home Secretary wide discretionary powers and these were used in December 1979 when it was decided that no work permits for overseas domestic workers would be issued from January 1980.

Almost simultaneously, those same discretionary powers were used to allow domestics into Britain, but without work permits.

The current position is that:

1. Domestics employed by visitors are admitted as visitors on condition they leave the country with their employers;

2. People entering the United Kingdom to live may bring with them domestic servants who have worked for them abroad for 12 months or more;

3. Domestic workers are not allowed to leave the service of the employer with whom they entered the country;

4. Unsurprisingly, the policy of not issuing work permits to domestics, but allowing them to work on visitors' visas, causes some confusion amongst immigration officials. Their recourse is to use both the work prohibited and employment-restricted-to-one employer stamps. It is a lottery as to which stamp the incoming domestic worker receives.

A Home Office official has informed the Anti-Slavery Society that there 'are no figures for the number of domestic servants admitted each year with their employers as visitors, as such admissions cannot be identified separately'.

This statement has to be viewed with some scepticism. The Home Secretary, using his discretionary powers, can simply make an administrative decision that such information be compiled at the port of entry. Additionally, all visitors fill in landing cards which, for those who subsequently overstay their legal time, is a weapon in the armoury of deportation officials as they record the official date of entry. Furthermore, employers in countries overseas, such as those in the Middle East, need to apply to the local British embassy or consulate for a visa for all those intending to visit the United Kingdom.

The Immigration Act, particularly the Immigration Rules within the Act, contain no section dealing with domestic work. This is curious, for Britain, in common with many Western countries having a large female working population, is experiencing a demand for help in the home. The Home Office, by making concessions allowing overseas visitors to bring in their domestic servants, is implicitly recognising this need.

In 1988 a second Immigration Act was passed which took away the right of appeal in deportation cases. This, combined with the fact that desperately poor people made vulnerable by the mere fact of that poverty, by being treated as appendages of their employers, by rarely knowing what is stamped in their passports or whether their employer has renewed their permission to stay, by being unable legally to change employer, has produced an intolerable but legal situation where the power is totally in the hands of the employer and the status of the employee is frequently reduced to that of a contemporary slave.

The Anti-Slavery Society is indebted to the two sister organisations working with domestics in Britain, Kalayaan and the Commission for Filipino Migrant Workers, which are co-operating extensively in the Society's research, and which, out of their intimate involvement with the victims of domestic service, have provided the following information:

A) The domestics come from a variety of Third World countries: Bangladesh, Brazil, Colombia, Ethiopia, Eritrea, India, Indonesia, Morocco, Nepal, Nigeria, Philippines, Sierra Leone and Sri Lanka.

B) The employers are drawn from Gulf and Middle Eastern states, from Greece, Hong Kong, India, Italy, Nigeria, Singapore, USA and UK.

The tragic case of Laxmi Swami is atypical on two counts:
domestic slaves do not receive justice and compensation, and most of them do not come from India. The overwhelming majority, perhaps in excess of 90 per cent of overseas domestic workers in Britain, are Filipinas.[1] What does seem to be true is that employers originating from abroad come, as did Mrs Swami's captors, from the Gulf.[2]

The Home Office has admitted that the authorities do not know how many overseas domestics are working in the United Kingdom. Based on the number of known runaways, or overstayers as they are also called, there must be a considerable community. For the last five years an average of 100 female domestic workers has run away from their employers every year. Each one of them knows of two or three captive servants. So it is not improbable that since the decision not to issue work permits ten years ago between 2,000 and 3,000 domestic workers have suffered conditions amounting to slavery in one western country alone. This figure does not include those overseas workers who are content at work.

Typically, an overseas domestic is a single Filipina in her 20s with financial responsibilities to her siblings who are continuing their education, or an older woman in her 30s and sometimes 40s who is trying to bring up a family with little or no help. Not infrequently they are widows.

They mainly find jobs through recruitment agencies in Manila and their first employment is usually in the Gulf area. No matter their skills and experience, the women overwhelmingly become servants, for domestic work is the easiest to get. They are not infrequently duped, being promised the work of their choice only to find on arrival that the employer gives them no choice - or rather the non-choice of returning home immediately at their own expense. Poverty drove them abroad in the first place and many of them land virtually with no money.

An aspect of the recruiting process that the Anti-Slavery Society intends to look at in detail is what seems to amount to debt bondage. Many of the women fall into debt by borrowing at exorbitant interest rates to pay recruitment fees, or by taking an advance payment from the recruiter. Before they can even begin to send money to their families – the prime purpose of working overseas – they have to redeem these debts.

After a year or two, and frequently without a visit home, the women are brought to London and the pattern of their working life is repeated. Their passport is kept by their employer, they are not allowed off the premises except rarely and then under some sort of supervision, they are ill treated and humiliated - slapping, hair pulling, being spat upon, being called dog, donkey, and sometimes slave are common - pay is either withheld or given months in arrears, food is what is left over from the meals of employers or their children, speaking to other servants is discouraged and sometimes forbidden. Their bed may be on the floor of the children's room, in a corridor, in the bathroom or in the kitchen. And of course, there is no respite. They are the first up in the mornings and the last to go to bed at night and even then their few hours of sleep may be interrupted. Sexual harassment is usual and rape is not unknown. They cannot legally change their jobs.

These conditions are those of slavery.

Those courageous women who do, and often at great physical risk, run away from their captors, immediately put themselves on the outside of the law. They cannot legally seek employment, they cannot overstay whatever period may be stamped in their passport, which in the majority of cases is in the employer's safe, and the appeal rights they have against deportation orders are very limited. In addition, they are frequently penniless and alone in a city they know only from the airport and the house they were confined to.

Case studies of modern domestic slaves in three countries are appended to illustrate the universality of the exploitation.[3]

The Anti-Slavery Society considers the stipulation that an employee cannot change employer to run counter to the last two centuries of British employer-employee relationships, custom and accepted practice.

It further regards the effects of the Immigration Acts as they touch upon overseas domestic workers, the non-issuance of work permits to these workers, and the effective treatment of these workers by the immigration authorities as appendages of the employer rather than as individuals in their own right, to be responsible for the servitude these domestics suffer in Britain. The Home Office, however inadvertently, is supporting slavery.

The Anti-Slavery Society recommends that the Home Office gives some consideration to the following measures;

1. the criminalisation of runaway domestic workers cease;
2. the permit system for overseas domestic workers be re-introduced;

3. such permits be issued to the employee and not to the employer;

4. the restoration of the right to change employers within the work category to be given to the overseas domestics;

5. the right of settlement within the United Kingdom be given to overseas domestic workers after four years of employment.

1 This figure was based on information available at the time; Kalayaan and CFMW now believe the percentage of Filipinas among overseas domestic workers in the UK is rather less.
2 New evidence shows that this is no longer the case as a number of employers have come from other countries for example: India, Hong Kong, Brunei, Brazil, and some African countries.
3 The case studies concerned three Filipinas: Alice, Sally and Sylvia; these are not repeated here, but Alice's story can be found in the main body of the text.

APPENDIX III

HOME OFFICE LEAFLET

HOME OFFICE IMMIGRATION ACT 1971

INFORMATION FOR DOMESTIC SERVANTS TRAVELLING TO THE UNITED KINGDOM

This leaflet explains..
the conditions of your stay in the United Kingdom and tells you where you can get advice about any problems which may arise while you are there.

Please read the leaflet carefully, keep it safe, and take it with you when you travel.

1. How long can I stay?

When you arrive in the United Kingdom and give your passport to the immigration officer he will stamp it telling you how long you can stay. This will normally be for 6 months if your employer is visiting the United Kingdom and for 12 months if he intends to live there for a longer period.

If you are granted entry for 6 months, and your employer stays longer than that, you can apply to the Home Office to extend your stay by successive periods of 12 months. The address to which you should apply is given in paragraph 8. If you remain in the United Kingdom with your employer for 4 years you will then be able to apply to remain in the United Kingdom indefinitely.

Your passport provides proof of your permission to enter or stay in the United Kingdom. It is an important document and you should keep it in a safe place.

2. What happens if my employer leaves the United Kingdom?

If you are accompanying your employer on a visit to the United Kingdom you will probably leave with him. If you stay longer you may not work unless members of his immediate family are also visiting and they wish you to work for them. You must leave before the end of the 6 month period in your passport.

If your employer is living in the United Kingdom you do not need to accompany him on trips abroad as long as he is still based in the United Kingdom and intends to return. If your employer leaves the United Kingdom permanently you will probably leave with him but if you stay you must not work for anybody else and you must leave before the end of the 12 month period in your passport.

If you are unsure about your right to remain in the United Kingdom and would like further advice, you should contact the Home Office – see paragraph 8.

3. Do I have the protection of the law against assault?
Everybody in the United Kingdom has the full protection of the criminal law, whatever their nationality or purpose of stay.

There are strict laws in the United Kingdom against assault. For example, criminal laws forbid :

Violence or violent behaviour
Keeping you shut indoors against your will
Sex without your consent

If anyone assaults you, go to the police. You can find their address and telephone number in the telephone book under "Police". In an emergency dial 999 and ask for the police. They will help you.

You can get general advice about your legal rights from your local Citizens' Advice Bureau – see paragraph 7 below.

4. Can I change my job?
No. The stamp placed in your passport by the Immigration Officer will record the name of your employer. You cannot work for anyone else. (But if after 4 years in the United Kingdom you have been given permission to remain there indefinitely you will then be free to change your employer if you wish)

5. What rights do I have if I loose my job?
If your contract of employment provides that your normal place of work for your employer is in the United Kingdom then you may qualify for limited protection under the United Kingdom's employment laws soon after you arrive. You may be entitled, for example, to at least one week's notice of dismissal. Other rights take longer to acquire. For example, if your employment has lasted for at least two years you may be able to claim unfair dismissal or qualify for a redundancy payment.

6. Can I stay in the United Kingdom if I no longer have a job?
Yes, if you have the money to support yourself, but you must leave before the end of the 6 month or 12 month period shown in your passport.

Remember you will be committing an offence if you take any other employment or overstay your time.

If you do not have the money or a ticket to enable you to return home you should contact your Embassy. The Embassy's address and telephone number are listed in the London telephone directory or can be obtained from Directory Enquiries by dialling 192.

7.[1] If you need advice about the law, medical treatment under the National Health Service, a welfare matter or on a problem connected with your employment you can contact your nearest Citizens' Advice Bureau. Their number is listed in the local telephone directory or can be obtained from Directory Enquiries by dialling 192. You can also get advice on immigration matters from

> The United Kingdom Immigrants Advisory Service
> 2nd Floor, County House
> 190 Great Dover Street
> London SE1 4BY
> Tel: 071 357 6917

8. Contacting the Home Office
You can contact the Home Office Immigration Department by telephone on 081-686 0688 during office hours or by writing to

> The Home Office Immigration Department
> Lunar House
> Wellesley Road
> Croydon CR9 2BY

or by attending in person at the above address where the Public Enquiry Office is open between 9.00a.m. and 4.00p.m. Monday to Friday.

---

1. Editors' note: this paragraph in the original leaflet has no number or title.

APPENDIX IV

Immigration and Nationality Department

Lunar House 40 Wellesley Road
Croydon CR9 2BY
Telephone 081-760 2757
(GTN 3822)

2 6 JAN 1993

Your reference	
Our reference	IMG/929/152/311
Date	25 January 1993

Mr Don O'Hara
Anti-Slavery International
180 Brixton Road
LONDON
SW9 6AT

Dear Mr O'Hara

Thank you for your enquiry of 20 January 1993.

The general position under the Immigration Rules is that overseas nationals (other than European Community nationals) coming to work here must have a work permit before setting out. The employer has to apply to the Department of Employment which administers the work permit scheme. Permits are not issued for unskilled or semi-skilled work and thus anyone coming to the United Kingdom for employment as a domestic will not normally qualify.

The Home Office recognises that this might cause difficulties for families coming to this country who wish to bring with them their domestic servants who have lived and worked with the family for some time. Therefore as a concession outside the Immigration Rules domestic servants engaged for household duties abroad may be admitted to the United Kingdom in certain circumstances.

The concession operates in 2 ways. Domestics accompanying an employer who is visiting the United Kingdom will themselves have their stay here limited to 6 months. Domestics accompanying an employer coming to take up residence here are admitted for 12 months in the first instance, but if the employer wishes to stay longer they may remain with him. Although leave to enter or stay is given to a domestic worker in line with the employer, he or she may stay here for the period granted irrespective of whether the employer leaves the country in the meantime. This is because once the decision has been taken to grant leave to enter or to stay in the United Kingdom, the period of leave is specifically given to the domestic worker as an individual distinct from the employer. Moreover, after 4 years working for the employer domestic workers become eligible to apply for settlement, at which point the restrictions and conditions on their stay are removed. We are, however, not prepared to allow domestic workers the freedom to seek and take up alternative employment here while their stay here is subject to conditions. To do so would not be in the interests of the resident labour force nor would it be fair to the many unskilled workers in developing countries excluded from the UK labour market. Thus if either the employer or the employee terminates the employment, for whatever reason, the employee has no entitlement to take other work here. It is not the case that domestics somehow have less rights here than other overseas workers. Everyone in the United Kingdom,

LH1.6

regardless of their nationality or purpose of stay, is entitled to the full protection of the criminal laws and can complain to the police if they are physically abused or are in any way deprived of their liberty. Subject to certain residential qualifications overseas workers are also entitled to benefit from our employment laws. Domestics admitted under the concession are no exception.

Nevertheless, we are sympathetic to the argument that overseas domestics are more vulnerable to exploitation than other groups of workers. That is why we have recently introduced new arrangements for their admission. These arrangements limit admission to domestics aged 17 or over who have worked for pay with the employer abroad for a substantial period - 12 months where the employer is coming as a visitor and 24 months otherwise. In all cases the domestic must obtain an entry clearance before setting out and the entry clearance officer will interview her in order to satisfy himself that the age and employment criteria are met. The entry clearance officer will also ensure that the domestic receives and understands an information leaflet explaining her rights. A copy of the leaflet will also go to the employer, under cover of a separate letter explaining its purpose. Copies of both the leaflet and the letter are enclosed.

We trust that these new arrangements will help to minimise the scope for abuse of domestics by their employers and meet the concerns that expresses.

Yours sincerely

R. Clifford.

LH1.6

APPENDIX V

THE EUROPEAN COMMUNITY

The European Parliament
Has directly elected members from each EC country and debates proposals for change in EC laws and resolutions on particular areas. It can investigate particular areas and produce reports. In practice it has very little power other than to recommend changes.

The European Commission
The executive cum civil service of the EC. It has 17 appointed members and drafts EC legislation. It produces EC regulations and directives for discussion by the European Parliament.

The Council of Ministers
The legislative body, consisting of Ministers from all EC countries. Having taken into account the views of the European Parliament it is up to the Council of Ministers to make the final decisions.

The European Court of Justice
Decides on legal cases brought under EC law.

APPENDIX VI

KALAYAAN: Model Contract of Employment for Domestic Workers.

KALAYAAN (FREEDOM)

JUSTICE FOR OVERSEAS DOMESTIC WORKERS

C/O C.F.M.W.
St. Francis Centre
Pottery Lane
W11 4NQ

Tel: 071- 221 6601
Fax: 071- 792 3060

Contract of Employment

Wages: Basic pay is £.......... per week to be paid on .... of the week.

Hours: A maximum 10 hour day with 1 hour for lunch and 2 x ½ hour breaks.

Overtime Rates:

For hours worked over and above the normal 10 hour day an overtime rate of £...............is to be paid.

Days Off: A minimum of 1½ days off per week. Sunday being the full day off and ½ a day taken during the week.

Sundays are only to be worked in special circumstances. If it is required a premium rate of £......... per hour is to be paid.

Holidays & Bank Holidays:

For every 1 month of service there is to be 1½ days paid holiday to be taken with mutual agreement.

Bank Holidays to be worked with a special rate of time and a half or one day off in lieu.

Sickness: In the event of sickness payment to be made as normal for a minimum of 2 weeks per annum.

Notice Period: To terminate employment a notice period of 1 week to be given by both parties.

Note: When the employer is away payments must be made at the same rate as the rest of the year.

Duties & Responsibilities:............................
....
....
....
....
....
....

Signed By Employer......................................

Signed By Employee.....................................

Adress..
....
....
Telephone Number:........................

KALAYAAN

Kalayaan takes its name from the Pilipino word meaning Freedom. It was formed in 1987 as an independent coalition of people and organisations who wanted to fight for the restoration of basic workers rights to overseas domestic workers and for an end to their current irregular legal status. It draws its members from migrant and immigrant support organisations, trade unions, law centres and concerned individuals.

Kalayaan's careful selection of responsible media outlets has produced accurate as well as widespread coverage of the issue, and this has won enormous public sympathy for the campaign. Building on this, Kalayaan's intense lobbying in the Houses of Parliament resulted in the all-party support of 104 MP's and a debate in the House of Lords in which all speakers (except the Government's) broadly supported Kalayaan's views. The campaign has also won the support of Church leaders, trade unions, human rights organisations, Black and other community organisations, and refugee and migrant groups.

Kalayaan also concerns itself with the practical needs of the workers. It helps workers forced to flee violence or exploitation by assisting them to find emergency housing, and by enabling them to get good legal advice so that they can make informed decisions. Kalayaan runs English classes in association with the Commission for Filipino Migrant Workers and the Brent Asian Women's Resource Centre, and also helps other groups and service agencies concerned with the welfare of migrant domestic workers. Kalayaan trains legal advisers, and provides legal support for the workers to obtain their unpaid wages, passports, and other belongings from former employers.

Kalayaan is currently being funded by the London Boroughs Grants Unit. All campaigning costs are raised through fund-raising activities and donations.

HOW YOU CAN HELP

Write to the Home Secretary and your local MP demanding an end to this form of slavery.

Help us to publicise this issue – we will be happy to send you more information, leaflets and petition forms.

Organise a public meeting in your community – we can supply speakers.

Affiliate to Kalayaan or make a donation to our funds.

PLEASE CONTACT:

The Secretary, Kalayaan,
c/o St Francis Centre, Pottery Lane, London W11 4NQ
Tel: 071-243 2942 Fax: 071-792 3060

Kalayaan's Briefing Papers

1 Briefing Paper in Relation to Domestic Workers (1993)
   Outlines the historical background to the campaign and discusses the legal aspect and solutions to the problem.

2 The Admission and Control of Overseas Domestic Workers in the UK
   Discusses legal points on the issue.

3 Background Paper for the 1990 Forum on Overseas Domestic Workers plus Resolutions Taken.

4 Position Paper (1987)
   Describes the immigration problems of a section of Filipino migrant domestic workers in Britain.

5 Kalayaan Briefing Notes Number 2
   Updates the story of the campaign.

6 Kalayaan's General Leaflet (1992)

Donations towards photocopying and postage will be welcome.

The following videos are available, on loan, for educational purposes:

BBC2 Open Space: *Domestic Slavery*, November 1987
GRANADA World in Action: *Britain's Secret Slaves*, July 1989
Pictures of Women/Channel 4: *Free Kuwait!* October 1992

Application for Affiliation

To
The Secretary
Kalayaan
St Francis Centre, Pottery Lane
London W11 4NQ

I have much pleasure in contributing to the funds of **Kalayaan**, Justice for Overseas Domestic Workers.
I enclose the sum of............pounds as a donation.
I enclose the sum of............pounds and wish to be affiliated.

Name ....
Address..
....

Affiliation Fees
National Organisations   £50
Regional Organisations   £20
Local and Voluntary Orgs   £15
Individuals   £5

Bankers Order

To Messrs..
Please pay to Bank of Ireland 30/32 Shepherd's Bush Green London W12 8RE to the credit of **Kalayaan** the sum of £.................... on.......................
and on .... in every succeeding year until otherwise ordered.

Signature...
Address..
....

This form, signed by the subscriber, should be forwarded to Kalayaan. Cheques and postal orders should be made payable to Kalayaan.

Anti-Slavery International

(Registered as a charity [no.214385] in the United Kingdom)
180 Brixton Road, London, SW9 6AT
Telephone: 071-582 4040; Fax: 071- 587 0573

As the methods of oppression have changed over the last two centuries, so the face of slavery has changed too. But the inability to withdraw one's labour is still the fundamental factor characterising the abuse of many millions of men, women and children, particularly, but not exclusively, those in the Third World.

The Anti-Slavery Society arose in 1839 out of the ashes of previous bodies opposed to enslavement. Now renamed Anti-Slavery International (ASI), it is the oldest international human rights organisation and the only one seeking to eliminate all forms of traditional and modern slavery.

The forms were codified by the United Nations in the 1956 Supplementary Convention on the Abolition of Slavery, the Slave Trade and Institutions and Practices Similar to Slavery. ASI is proud of its primary role in shaping the definitions of this international instrument.

ASI's purpose is the elimination of slavery in all its forms, through:
- research
- awareness raising
- lobbying of governments and international bodies
- public campaigning

all of which complement and support the efforts of groups in the UK and abroad with similar concerns. It also works for the rights of indigenous peoples.

ASI's main work today is concentrated on slavery; bonded labour; the oppression of women; and exploitative child labour.

Anti-Slavery International welcomes members. Annual membership: £15 (Canada and USA 30 dollars). Associate annual membership: £5. Life membership £200 (Canada and USA 400 dollars).

Publications from Anti-Slavery International

Human Rights Series

No.1   Western Sahara: the fight for self-determination. 1976
by John Gretton OUT OF PRINT

No.2   Equatorial Guinea: the forgotten dictatorship. 1976
by Suzanne Cronjé 75p

No.3   Eritrea – Africa's Longest War. 1980
by David Pool OUT OF PRINT

No.4   Debt Bondage – A Survey. 1981
by Judith Ennew £1.50

Child Labour Series (recent reports)

No.8   School Age Workers in Britain Today. 1987
by Caroline Moorhead £3.50

No.9   A Pattern of Slavery: India's Carpet Boys. 1990
£3.50

No.10   Children in Bondage: Slaves of the Subcontinent. 1991
£3.25

No.11   Kashmiri Carpet Children: Exploited Village Weavers. 1991
by Peter Cross £2

No.12   Child Workers in Portugal. 1992.
by Suzanne Williams £4.50

Indigenous Peoples and Development Series

No.3   Papua New Guinea: A False Economy. 1986
by Kenneth Good £4.95

No.6   West Papua: Plunder in Paradise. 1990
£4.95

Form of Application for Membership

To
The Director,
Anti-Slavery International,
180 Brixton Road, London SW9 6AT

I have much pleasure in contributing to the funds of **Anti-Slavery International** the sum of..pounds per annum and wish to be enrolled as a member.

Name..
Address...
....
....

Credit Card No..
Expiry Date...
Signature..

Bankers Order

To Messrs..
Please pay to Barclays Bank plc, 463 Brixton Road, London SW9 8HL, to the credit of **Anti-Slavery International**, the sum of
£............................ on.......................... and on...................... in every succeeding year until otherwise ordered.

Signature..
Address..
....
This form, signed by the subscriber, should be forwarded to ASI.

Cheques and postal orders should be made payable to Anti-Slavery International.

Deed of Covenant

I,..
of...

hereby Covenant with Anti-Slavery International of 180 Brixton Road, London SW9 6AT, that during the period of four years from the date hereof or during my life, whichever is the shorter period, I will pay to the Treasurer for the time being of the said society for the general use of Anti-Slavery International, such sum as will, after deduction of income tax, leave in the hands of Anti-Slavery International the net sum of .... such sum to be paid annually, the first payment to be made on the ....day of..19......................
Dated this..............................day of...............................19........

....(Signature)
Signed, Sealed and Delivered by the above-named in the presence of

Signature of Witness..
Address..
....
Occupation..

Anti-Slavery International is registered as a charity [no. 214 385] in the United Kingdom.